The Drama & Theatre Arts
Course Book

The
Drama &
Theatre Arts
Course
Book

David Self

Macmillan Education

First published 1981
Reprinted 1981 (twice), 1983 (twice), 1984, 1985, 1986

Published by
MACMILLAN EDUCATION LTD
Houndmills, Basingstoke, Hampshire RG21 2XS
and London
Companies and representatives
throughout the world

Printed in Hong Kong

British Library Cataloguing in Publication Data

Self, David
 The drama and theatre arts course book.
 1. Theatre
 I. Title
 792   PN2037
 ISBN 0-333-27596-9

Contents

5   Modern theatre

Acknowledgements

The author and publishers wish to thank the following who have kindly given permission for the use of copyright material:

Associated Book Publishers Ltd for an extract from *The Caretaker* by Harold Pinter published by Methuen and Co. Ltd Copyright © 1960 by Theatre Promotions Limited; Lesley Davies for her account of her first acting job; Faber and Faber Limited for extracts from *Rosencrantz and Guilderstern Are Dead* by Tom Stoppard; Samuel French Limited for an extract from *Streuth* from *Four Plays for Coarse Actors* edited by Michael Green; Hamish Hamilton Limited for *The Last Flower* by James Thurber from *Vintage Thurber*; the Headmaster on behalf of Bungay High School for an extract from *Ring-a-King*; Heinemann Educational Books Limited for an extract from *The Golden Masque of Agamemnon* by John Wiles; Oxford University Press for an extract from 'Smoking Is Bad For You' from *The Oxford Chekhov*, Volume I *Short Plays* translated and edited by Ronald Hingley (1968); Penguin Books Ltd for extracts from *Prometheus Bound* by Aeschylus, translated by Philip Vellacott (1961, Penguin Classics), and *The Canterbury Tales* by Chaucer translated by Neville Coghill (1951, Penguin Classics); Laurence Pollinger Limited on behalf of the Estate of the late Mrs Frieda Lawrence Ravagli for the poem 'Snake'· from *The Complete Poems of D. H. Lawrence*; Pressdram Limited for an extract from *Private Eye* magazine; Nigel Richardson for an extract from his play *Uppingham by the Sea*; Syndication International Limited for an extract from the *Daily Mirror*, 22 May 1972; Theatre Arts Books for an extract from *An Actor Prepares* by Konstantin Stanislavski.

Copyright © 1936 by Theatre Arts Inc. and 1948 by Elizabeth R. Hapgood.

The author and publishers wish to acknowledge the following photograph sources:

'Music Workshop – Pupil Pamphlet, Summer 1979' – BBC Publications p. 32; BBC Copyright Photo pp. 45, 49; BBC Hulton Picture Library pp. 33, 76; Mel Calman p. 67 right, originally in the 1978 Edinburgh Festival Official Programme; Camera Press p. 38; J. Allan Cash Limited p. 16; Cassell Limited pp. 26, 27, 85; Chester Gateway Theatre p. 90 top; Colorsport p. 39; Crown Copyright Reserved – Central Office Information p. 40; Douglas Dickins p. 23; T. Edmondson p. 111; EMI Records pp. 105, 106; Ronald Grant p. 94; Greater London Council p. 62; GTO Film Distributors p. 102; G. V. Hazlehurst pp. 30, 31, 37, 61 bottom, 95; Tom Holte p. 61 top; Marcel Imsana p. 99; Noeline Kelly p. 36; A. F. Kersting p. 42; Leichner of London pp. 46, 66, 86; Michael Lyell Associates p. 90 bottom; Mansell Collection pp. 41, 52, 67 left; Mander and Mitchenson Theatre Collection pp. 53, 71, 88; National Portrait Gallery, London pp. 54, 72, 73; National Tourist Organisation of Greece p. 13; Maurice Newcombe pp. 19, 59; Phaidon Press – Ms L. Laurie p. 14; Punch pp. 15, 56; Rank Strand Electric pp. 11, 25, 44, 65; Royal Shakespeare Company – John Napier p. 63; Shakespeare Birthplace Trust pp. 57, 58, 68, 103; Ronald Sheridan's Photo Library p. 24; Sutton Manor High School p. 20; Syndication International p. 97; Trans World Eye p. 110; Reg Wilson pp. 47, 70, 87, 98, 101, 104, 109; Drawing by Roy Castle. Reproduced from *The Complete Guide to Britain's National Theatre*; Heinemann £1.50 and by kind permission of the National Theatre. p. 92. Frontispiece: Queen Mary College/Martin Lipscombe

The cover photograph is from the Cockpit Arts Workshop production of John Wiles' *The Golden Masque of Agamemnou* (1977) by kind permission of the GLC Photographic Unit.

The publishers have made every effort to trace the copyright holders but if they have inadvertently overlooked any they will be pleased to make the necessary arrangements at the first opportunity.

Introduction

This book is offered as a basis for a one or two year course in theatre arts. It does not intend to be prescriptive but to offer an introduction to widely accepted and proven practice. It is hoped that it will serve as a first reference book and motivate various creative, academic and practical projects.

Some will wish to work through the book sequentially, spending a half or full term on each part. Others will wish to be more selective, using only those parts applicable to their particular syllabus – while others will wish to move from unit to unit as required by particular projects. Each part relates to a specific form of theatre:

1 Greek
2 Medieval
3 Shakespearean
4 Victorian
5 Modern

Within each part there are eighteen units on a recurring pattern:

.1 Stages
.2 Theatres
.3 Dramatists
.4 Improvisation
.5 Movement
.6 Speech
.7 Acting
.8 Mime/dance
.9 Directing
.10 Documentary
.11 Design
.12 Costume
.13 Lighting
.14 Sound
.15 Make-up
.16 Stagecraft
.17 FOH
.18 Project

The author hopes that his readers will accept the word 'actor' as including 'actress' and the pronoun 'he' as including 'she' where relevant.
Lastly he wishes to record his gratitude and affection for those who have worked with him on the productions and projects that have done so much to shape this book.

1

Greek Theatre

1.1 Stages: arena

All you need for drama is a space. An empty
space. It can be the middle of a room. A space
where two corridors meet. Or a street.
What sort of street entertainers can you think of?

Over the weeks, try developing your own
company of buskers, each with a different act.
Each busker should be able to perform his or her
act wherever there is an empty space and should
not need any special equipment. In this way, you
could build up a mobile entertainment that could
easily tour other schools, colleges or old people's
homes.

Think now of other empty spaces, or 'arenas',
that are used for staging events:

    boxing or wrestling ring

    sports stadium

    circus ring.

What have they in common. How is the
audience arranged? What is the relationship
between audience and performers? Is the
audience involved in the action? How? Why?

Many modern theatres are designed so that
the stage is 'in-the-round'. Study the
illustration below. What do you think will be the
advantages and problems of staging a play in
such an arena?

This is what happened in one school when, for the first time, they arranged the seating in their school hall 'in-the-round':

Our assembly hall seats nearly two hundred, and to our amazement we discovered that on re-arranging the chairs two deep around the perimeter of the room and by putting some of the chairs on the stage, nearly half the audience would have a front row seat. We erected a foot-high platform, painted a matt grey, occupying perhaps half of the central acting space; and built ramps to go at two of the corners. We left gangways among parts of the audience to allow actors to make their entrances and exits from varying parts of the hall.

Though we had done away with the need for scenery, and so saved much work, we found that great care would have to be given to the properties and costumes, as the audience was to be only three or four feet away from the action. Similarly make-up presented its problems – it being hard to age any boy appreciably and convincingly at such short range.

Note that as soon as you start performing in-the-round, there is a much greater immediacy. Like the audience at a boxing or wrestling match, the spectators are close to the action and become closely involved. They are eavesdroppers, looking at action that is going on in the midst of them.

Note too that on an arena stage the actors relate to each other, and do not *project* to an audience. This makes an arena stage very suitable for staging improvised scenes.

As you begin to develop your improvisation work, try presenting such scenes in a small circle formed by other members of your group. Also see 5.1.

1.2   Theatres: Greek

Unlike the intimacy of 'theatre-in-the-round', Greek theatres were built on an epic scale. Some, like the one at Epidavros, could seat about 20 000 spectators. NB Find out how many seats there are in your local theatre – and how many people can attend your nearest football ground.

Greek drama grew out of religious festivals. Ceremonies, involving songs and dances, were acted out in honour of the god Dionysus, but gradually stories about Dionysus were replaced by ones about other heroes and gods. Then monologues, recited by the leader of the chorus (*see below*), were added at certain points. These monologues provided religious and moral comment on the story. Violence and death always took place off stage and were reported to the audience by a messenger character.

Later, various dramatists added extra characters. All the actors wore masks to indicate their character, platform shoes to make them appear taller, and padded costumes to emphasise natural proportions. All this of course was necessary so that spectators far from the stage would see what was happening.

The earliest theatres consisted simply of a huge circle of seats carved into a hillside with a circular, flat area where the singers and dancers performed. This area was called the *orchestra*.

By the time of Sophocles and Euripides (see 1.3), this area was used by the chorus and chorus leader, who sang and spoke their comments on the action. The actors stood behind the orchestra, possibly on a slightly raised platform. In the early years of Greek theatre, the actors performed against a background of open countryside, or the sea. Then it became usual to build a changing room for the actors behind the stage. This was known as the *skene* and the acting platform was called the *pro-skenion* – literally: 'in front of the *skene*'. From this, we get our word '*proscenium*'.

By the end of the fifth century BC, the *skene* usually had an upper storey, the *episkenion*, from which could be operated some sort of crane that would permit gods and goddesses to descend from, and return to, 'heaven'. It would almost certainly have been used in the play *Peace* by Aristophanes (see 1.10). The *skene* became a kind of scenery and was used to represent houses, palaces or any kind of building. Actors could appear at windows in the upper storey, 'watchmen' could stand on the roof, etc.

There were ramps at either side of the stage by which actors could enter and exit. The whole acting area was separated from the auditorium by two corridors or passageways, the *parodos*.

Though Greek theatres were enormous by modern standards, they had excellent acoustics – the hillside amplifying the sound naturally. If you visit the remains of the theatres at Epidavros

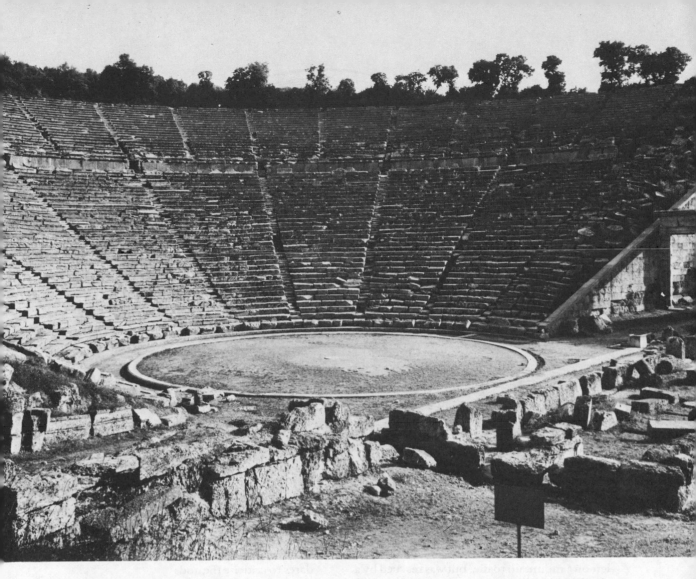

or Delphi, you can prove this for yourself. If you stand on the 'stage' and talk in a normal but distinct voice, you will be heard at the farthest points of the auditorium. Discover the derivation of the word, *auditorium*.

Since 1954, regular performances of classical plays have once again been given at Epidavros (see above).

1.3 Greek dramatists

The diagram overleaf is a plan of the theatre at Epidavros. This is the only one that survives that is really like those used by the classic Greek playwrights.

Among the many writers of the classic period of Greek theatre, 500–300 BC, four are especially famous.

Aeschylus (525–456 BC)

He is generally said to be the founder of European drama and it is thought he wrote some ninety plays. Only seven, all tragedies, survive. Among these is *Prometheus Bound*. Unit 1.18 gives you the chance to devise your own play based on the story of this tragedy.

He also wrote a famous trilogy – a group of three related plays, known as *The Oresteia* which is about Agamemnon and his family and their crimes against the gods.

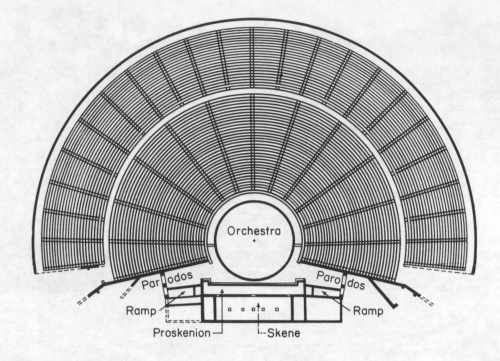

Orchestra

Par|odos   Par|odos

Ramp   Ramp

Proskenion   Skene

Sophocles (496–406 BC)

Like Aeschylus, Sophocles wrote many plays – but again only seven survive, and they are all tragedies.

He too wrote a trilogy. It is about Oedipus, son of Laius the king of Thebes. A prophecy said Laius would be killed by his own son, so he ordered the destruction of his son. Oedipus was left on a mountain to die, but was rescued by a shepherd. Oedipus grew up, not knowing who his real parents were, and killed Laius.

He then went to Thebes which was ruled by Creon, brother of Jocasta – Oedipus' mother. Thebes was plagued by a monster, the Sphinx. Creon offered the kingdom and the hand of Jocasta in marriage to whoever could rid Thebes of the monster. Oedipus succeeded, won the kingdom and married his mother. They had two sons and two daughters, including Antigone. When they found out what had happened, Oedipus put out his own eyes and Jocasta hanged herself.

The three plays that form the trilogy are *Oedipus at Colonus*, *Oedipus Rex* ('Oedipus the King') and *Antigone*.

Euripides (484–406 BC)

His plays are very much more realistic and more 'modern' than those of Aeschylus and Sophocles. Men and women are represented very much more as they are in everyday life, but the ending is often solved by a 'deus ex machina' (see 1.2). Eighteen of his ninety-two plays survive. Unlike the earlier Greek tragedians, he dares to criticise the gods.

Aristophanes (448–380 BC)

Unlike Aeschylus, Sophocles and Euripides, Aristophanes wrote comedies. Eleven of his forty plays survive complete. Some of them are very rude indeed. One famous one is *Lysistrata* in which the women of Greece refuse to sleep with their husbands until the war between Athens and Sparta is ended. Another of his comedies about the same war is the play called *Peace* (see 1.10).

Two of his most famous plays are *The Frogs* which is about Euripides and Aeschylus, in the afterlife, fighting for a prize to show who is the best writer of tragedies; and *The Birds*, a political satire set in 'cloud-cuckoo-land'.

1.4 Improvisation: acceptance

The first rule of improvisation is that it must be built on acceptance, and never on conflict. Critics may write that the essence of drama is conflict, but the director in the theatre knows that his production will be more successful and 'happier' if his actors are co-operating rather than competing on stage (see 1.7).

This is especially so when improvising. Rejecting ideas leads only to a kind of stalemate:

A I see there's a lot of apples on your trees this
  year.
B There isn't.
A Oh . . . I thought there was.
B No.
A Oh . . .

It's hard to rescue such a scene. Now imagine this improvisation:

A I see there's a lot of apples on your trees this
  year.
B Yes. Yes, there are.
A What are you going to do with them?
B Pick them.
A Yes, obviously. But then what?
B Well . . .

When B accepts the opening line, the improvisation can progress. When it is rejected, there is stale-mate.

In pairs, improvise conversations from these starting lines. Take it in turns to be A and B – and always 'accept' the opening line:

I see you're keeping giraffes in your back garden.
I hear you've just won the pools.
I hear you've got a single in the charts.
You're very intelligent, aren't you?
I hear you're going to enter the Miss World competition.
Headmaster, was it absolutely necessary to expel my son?
What's it like being Prime Minister?
Have you always wanted to be a film star?
Do you enjoy having your own television show?

Now play scenes between a door-to-door salesman and an inquisitive but hard-up housewife. The salesman is demonstrating, and trying to sell, either:
a) clockwork mice that pick up crumbs, dust, etc.
b) motor-powered roller skates or
c) permanent make-up.

Improvise a scene based on this cartoon.

MANNERS AND MODES.
STUDY OF A WIFE REVENGING HERSELF ON A HUSBAND WHO HAS PERSISTENTLY CONDEMNED THE MODERN FASHIONS.

15

Involve the whole group in a party scene. Decide who is to be host. Let everyone keep their real name, but as they arrive at the party, the host will introduce them to others and announce the incredibly wonderful things they have just achieved: 'Joe, this is Amanda – her new novel has just been filmed'; 'Sarah, do you know Peter – you perhaps saw his show on ITV last night?' You must not deny your achievement, and as you circulate at the party, you should try to find out as much as possible about the other guests, and flatter them as sincerely as possible.

1.5   Movement exercises

Movement indicates:
  character;
  mood and attitude;
  reactions;
  the inner man, what a person is thinking, what he *is*.

Movement on stage must communicate such points to the audience. But movement must be realistic and natural, not exaggerated – except for comic purposes. Movement must be controlled, intentional – but easy and fluid.

The good actor is the one that looks at home in his environment, as though he *belongs* in that setting.

Every actor needs to undertake movement exercises, not just when training but regularly.

1.   Use lively Tijuana-type music for this exercise: stand up and face away from the rest of the group; look at your thumbs; begin moving them to the music; now move fingers, hands, arms, shoulders, head. Keep those moving in time to the music. Begin also to move the knees, spine – now move away from the spot and move around with the music. Keep arms, shoulders, spine moving.
2.   Choose a spot some distance away. Move to it in slow motion. Lower yourself to the floor in slow motion. Slowly get up again and repeat. Undertake everyday actions in slow motion.
3.   Practise moving to different percussion rhythms.
4.   Each time a cymbal is struck, move in one of

these ways, which could be called out by the leader of the group:
  stretch; turn, reach, bend, curl, rise, drift, coil, spread, shrink, crouch, stretch, fade, flop, rest.
Repeat in slow motion.
5.   Now work on these lines from D. H. Lawrence's poem *Snake*, and in slow, controlled movements, bring the scene to life:

*He reached down from a fissure in the earth-wall in the
    gloom
And trailed his yellow-brown slackness soft-bellied
    down, over the edge of the stone trough
And rested his throat upon the stone bottom,
And where the water had dripped from the tap, in a small
    clearness,
He sipped with his straight mouth,
Softly drank through his straight gums, into his slack long
    body,
Silently . . .
He lifted his head from his drinking, as cattle do,
And looked at me vaguely, as drinking cattle do,
And flickered his two-forked tongue from his lips, and
    mused a moment . . .
He drank enough
And lifted his head, dreamily, as one who has drunken,
And flickered his tongue like a forked night on the air, so
    black,
Seeming to lick his lips,
And looked around like a god, unseeing, into the air,
And slowly turned his head,
And slowly, very slowly, as if thrice adream,
Proceeded to draw his slow length curving round
And climb again the broken bank of my wall-face.*

1.6 Speech: diction

It is not enough for an actor to be realistic. He must be heard by his audience, and this means taking care over the delivery of his lines. It does not mean aiming at a false, artificial style of delivery; it does mean ensuring that the sound of the voice travels.

Breath comes from the lungs. It is given sound by the vocal cords and resonance by the pharynx, mouth and nasal cavity. The tongue's shape and movements; the hard and soft palates; the teeth, jaw and lips all combine to produce different sounds.

Get in the habit of breathing deeply, steadily and slowly – especially before beginning a scene. When delivering a speech, don't trap the sound by letting the head droop. Don't force the sound from the back of the throat and don't shout. Instead, make the lips, tongue and jaw do the work. Take special care in shaping words with the lips. Speak from the front of the mouth; make the jaw work. Open the mouth – use it to propel the sound through the auditorium.

This speech comes from *Prometheus Bound* by Aeschylus (see 1.3). Prometheus has been bound to a rock as a punishment for defying the gods and giving the gift of fire to mankind (see 1.18). Imagine yourself to be Prometheus and deliver this speech to the mountainside!

Prometheus: O divinity of sky, and swift-winged winds, and leaping streams,
  O countless laughter of the sea's waves,
  O Earth, mother of all life!
  On you, and on the all-seeing circle of the sun, I call:
  See what is done by gods to me, a god!

  See with what outrage
  Racked and tortured
  I am to agonize
  For a thousand years!
  See this shameful prison
  Invented for me
  By the new master of the gods!
  I groan in anguish
  For pain present and pain to come:
  Where shall I see rise
  The star of my deliverance?

What am I saying? I know exactly every thing
That is to be; no torment will come unforeseen.
My appointed fate I must endure as best I can.
Knowing the power of Necessity is irresistible.
Under such suffering, speech and silence are alike
Beyond me. For bestowing gifts upon mankind
I am harnessed in this torturing clamp. For I am he
Who hunted out the source of fire, and stole it,
    packed
In pith of a dry fennel-stalk. And fire has proved
For men a teacher in every art, their grand resource.
That was the sin for which I now pay the full price,
Bared to the winds of heaven, bound and crucified.

You may wish to use this speech, or the ideas
contained in it, when working on unit 1.18.

Now tackle the more difficult task of
delivering the lines from D. H. Lawrence's
poem, *Snake*, in such a way that your delivery
matches the mood of the poem but can also be
heard throughout the hall or auditorium.

1.7 Acting: co-operation

There are many stories, some of them very
funny, about professional actors not keeping to
the script or to their moves – either to make each
other laugh at a serious moment or to 'upstage'
each other.

On leaving school, Lesley Davies got a job as
Student Assistant Stage Manager in a small
theatre. After a few weeks she was given a small
part in a play.

It was a costume play and I had a long dark red
velvet dress to wear. I had nothing to do during
most of the play but there was one good bit where I
sat on a couch right at the front of the stage with the
old character lady while she told me all her guilty
secrets. It was her scene really – I only had about
four lines but I was playing it very gormless and
getting a few laughs even in rehearsal.

Anyway on the first night I wasn't half as shaky
as I thought I'd be. My big scene was the first in the
second act and sitting there on the couch with the
character lady waiting for the curtain I just felt very
excited. Then the curtain rose and she said her first
line. As I started to reply she got up, walked to the
back of the couch and played the whole scene
pacing distractedly across the stage behind me. I
didn't know what to do. You've got to look at
somebody when your talking to them. I couldn't
say my lines straight to the audience. If she'd kept

still I would have gone and stood next to her but she
was moving all the time and I couldn't very well
chase her round the stage. I had to spend my entire
big scene with my neck twisted round and my back
to the audience. I felt terrible.

I even thought of going round to her dressing-
room and begging her not to do it the next night,
but I knew it wouldn't do any good. The next day
one of the actors was in the kitchen while I was
making the tea so I had a long moan to him about it.
He wasn't very sympathetic, just shrugged his
shoulders and said that I was the only one who
could stop her getting up.

I thought about it all day but I didn't really cotton
on to what he meant until the very moment when I
was once again sitting next to her on the couch
waiting for the curtain. Then it struck me like a
flash of lightning. Of course I could stop her. As the
curtain went up I stuck my foot down hard on her
dress where it trailed on the floor, and grabbed
some folds of material in my left hand which was
out of sight of the audience. She said her first line
and started to get up. I held on for dear life. She
looked down, saw what I was doing and tried a
quick pull but I wouldn't let go so after glaring at
me she gave in and we played the scene just as we'd
rehearsed it. I'd won. Then I remembered I was
only the student ASM. All she had to do was
complain to the director afterwards and I'd
probably get the sack. I wished I hadn't done it.
Then she suddenly dropped her fan and as she
leaned down to pick it up she whispered
something. I couldn't believe my ears. 'Good girl,'
she said. 'You're learning fast.'

Although such stories *are* funny and although
you have got to learn to stick up for yourself,
good acting results when the actors are co-
operating, not fighting against each other. For
example, Cleopatra can only play her big scene if
her maid-servants are playing their part too.

Let one actor or actress sit or stand upstage.
Without that person changing their attitude or
position, the other members of the group enter,
two by two, and form a tableau to make the
central character appear to be:
  a dictator;
  an outcast;
  a popular person;
  a criminal.
Now repeat the tableaux, but involve all three
players in each scene. Remember: good acting
involves the co-operation of all those on stage –
it cannot be left to the central character in a

scene. But remember too: don't overact so that you direct attention to the wrong character or upstage a fellow actor.

Acting requires trust and sympathy. Get a partner and stand facing him or her. Choose a subject and then make a speech on that subject, each partner speaking alternate words. This is a good exercise in mind-reading!

NB Remember that a production requires co-operation between actors and all the technical staff as well!

1.8 The four elements

The ancient Greeks believed there were four elements: earth, water, fire and air.

Try developing movements that illustrate these elements.

Earth

Half close your eyes, let your shoulders droop. You are heavy, able to take only one plodding step at a time. You look around with suspicion and envy; you sulk. You are made of earth, hardly able to find the energy to raise your arm. All your movements are lumbering, literally 'down to earth'. Made of earth, you try to come close to the earth.

Water

Like a mountain stream, your movements are rapid and easy, swirling, flexing, falling. But soon you join up with others, tributaries merging to form a mature river – swaying, flowing calmly, meandering. You move along sedately, proudly; an unhurried stately but fluid procession.

Fire

First a flame, growing from the floor, turning, reaching, curling, rising, wavering, flickering, sinking, fading, dying. Next a fire, a group of flames. Rooted to the spot at first, some working close to the floor, others reaching up to feed on air; gradually coming to life, gaining strength and then spreading, seeking to devour all that is within reach.

Air

Air is light-hearted, free and easy, the eternal optimist. It moves gently, slowly but cheerfully; it moves with a whistle or a whisper, with the ease of an athlete filmed in slow motion, hardly touching the ground.

Improvise music to accompany your movements or find suitable recorded music to illustrate each element.

Improvise and then develop encounters between the elements. What will happen when fire meets air? When fire meets water? When water meets earth?

Develop a dance of the elements – or one that expresses a conflict of emotions that might be included in a project on the Greek theatre. You might, for example, dance a mime of a Greek hero triumphing over an unseen foe, a mime of welcome for a returning hero or a dance of death – a lament for a dead or dying hero (see above).

1.9 The script

'Titles' at the end of a television play or near the beginning of a film include 'credits' to all the various people who have worked on that production, from the executive producer to the property master, from the designer to the costume makers. One of the credits will be to the writer. Much of what we see will have been decided by what he wrote. But the film or television play is far more than the invention of one man or woman.

The director has influenced it a lot by deciding where certain scenes should be 'shot' and how they were to be acted. The way the designer planned the sets will have influenced what appears on the screen. The casting director's choice of a rugged, bronzed actor rather than someone who is 'pale and interesting' to play the hero will alter our reactions. Similarly the film will be altered if the leading lady is a bouncy blonde rather than a fair young innocent! The cutting from one scene to another, the lighting, the music, the sound effects and many other features all contribute to the final production. There will have been a chance for many people to share their ideas, but usually it is the director who is in charge and who makes the final decisions. So it is with a stage play.

Some directors have very strong ideas of their own and their production turns out very differently to what the writer might have expected. He might be pleased, surprised or horrified. Alternatively the director might take great trouble to ensure that the production is as close as possible to what the writer first imagined.

20

(The house lights go down.
A sudden crack of thunder that is not quite thunder, which echoes and re-echoes through the hall. Before the sound has died...
Mist creeps across the floor. A smell of incense from the tripod.
The music starts, an eerie sound that might be wailing accompanied by a single drumbeat that resembles the dripping of water or perhaps it is the dripping of water. The main **cast** *enters in two lines and takes its place around the perimeter, kneeling on the floor. The actors lift their arms and link them. They start a rhythmical swaying which grows more abandoned as they struggle to speak. The sound we hear is not a pleasant one; it is as if they are trying to force it out between locked jaws.)*

Girls   Mm-mm-mm-mm...

Boys   Ga-ga-ga-ga-ga...

(The music builds like a wind rising. The struggle to say the word drives the actors to their feet. Now they stamp and begin to move more wildly. Their agony is doubled. The lights and mist go red. Now it looks like blood spilling across the floor. The music rises to a climax. As it breaks with a loud chord, the actors triumphantly explode with the cry –)

All   Aga-mem-non!

(Silence)

A script is not a complete play. Whether we are going to produce it on stage or on tape, imagine it as a film, or simply read it, we must take on the roles of director, designer, stage manager and actors to see how it can emerge from being a script into that living thing – a play.

A play is something to listen to. The plot, the ideas, the speeches are written down. The playwright has presented us with that half. But a play is also something to watch. And that means actions, expressions, costumes and scenery, lighting and sound effects – which are for us to imagine and perhaps to put into effect.

If we are to be fair to the writer, we must first think hard about what he wanted to say, and how we can lift his ideas off the page. Of course, we can add ideas of our own but these will only have a point if they follow an understanding of the play's message.

The following is the opening stage direction of a modern play by John Wiles about the Greek hero, Agamemnon (see 1.3). Discuss the effects the author wants on stage and how you could achieve them. What dangers must you avoid? What properties and effects will you need? Try working on the scene.

Later you could perhaps adapt some of the ideas you have developed in this unit and incorporate them in other projects.

1.10 Documentary: War and Peace

In 1963 a famous director, Joan Littlewood, and her company, Theatre Workshop, created a very successful documentary play, *Oh What a Lovely War!* This show used traditional World War I songs, slides, revue sketches, a newspanel and dance routines. As the programme said, 'Everything spoken during this evening either happened or was said, sung or written during 1914–1918.'

Besides being very entertaining, this was a savage attack on the stupidity of war and bad leadership. 'In 1960 an American Military Research Team fed all the facts of World War I into the computers they use to plan World War III. They reached the conclusion that the 1914–1918 war was impossible and couldn't have happened. There could not have been so many blunders nor so many casualties.' Certainly there were many examples of thousands of men being sacrificed to gain a few hundred yards of mud.

Oh What a Lovely War! was of course a satire. The war was anything but 'lovely' and the sarcastic singing of popular songs of the day, while showing slides of the real horror, made a striking impact in the theatre.

Try researching, compiling and staging your own documentary on a topic you feel strongly about. It could be an historical event, an environmental problem, a social problem or a topical or local issue. You will find help in reference books; the local or school college library; in old letters and newspapers; and from those who remember or feel strongly about the issue.

You might use improvised and scripted scenes, slides, special sound and lighting effects, piano and percussion, posters, rostra blocks, mime, debate and songs. See if you can convince your audience of your viewpoint!

In 421 BC the Greek writer Aristophanes pointed out the stupidity of war by writing a comedy called *Peace*.

Trygaeus, an elderly farmer, is being ruined by the war between Athens and Sparta. He decides to go up to heaven to see the gods and persuade them to stop the war by returning Peace, a statue of a very beautiful woman, to earth. Eventually Trygaeus gets to heaven on the back of a gigantic beetle – only to find that

Zeus is so disgusted with man that he has gone off on holiday leaving Hermes behind as caretaker of Heaven. War has moved in, along with his assistant, Havoc.

Eventually Trygaeus and his slave rescue Peace, together with the even more beautiful Harvest and Festival, and return to earth. Such characters as the helmet maker and the arms salesman are furious that Peace has returned, but the story ends with much rejoicing and Greek dancing. So the plot goes – more or less . . .

To improvise the story, you will need the following characters: Trygaeus, his slave, Hermes, War, Havoc, Harvest, Festival, the helmet maker and the arms salesman. You could include other farmers and their wives, a second slave and a spear-maker; and Peace could be played by an actress instead of being a statue.

This is how it might begin:

(Enter the slave)

Slave *(to the audience)*   That creature! Can you hear it? What an appetite it's got, munching away there! It's a full-time job feeding it, I'm quite exhausted! I'd better go and see if it's finished. *(Looks off stage)* Cor, it's eating fit to bust! *(Imitating)* munch, munch, munch! I've never seen anything like it! It's about the size of a small donkey. It's certainly the biggest beetle I've ever seen. *(Pause)* You what? Yes, that's what I said – a beetle. Honest, a very big beetle. It belongs to my master. *(Pause)* What? You want me to explain? Well, I'm a slave. I've not got a name. I'm just a slave. I live in Athens, and my master is an old fool – I mean, a nice old gentleman called Trygaeus. He's a farmer. He grows vines and makes the grapes into wine. Well, the thing is, Trygaeus is mad. What he does is, all day long he stares up at the sky with his mouth wide open – like this *(demonstrates)* and he complains and complains and moans and moans to Zeus. Zeus? You know who Zeus is?
Well he *is* the king of the gods isn't he. Now where was I? Oh yes, my master. 'Zeus,' he says, 'what are you trying to do? Zeus, what are you trying to do to all our people?' Hey quiet a moment, I think I hear something.

Trygaeus *(off stage)*   Zeus, what are you trying to do to all our people?

1.11   Design: backdrops

Greek drama, as we have seen (unit 1.2), was originally performed against a natural background – the open countryside. In later years the *skene* provided an anonymous background that could represent almost any building. The same effect was achieved in the Elizabethan playhouse (see 3.2) where the inner and upper stages provided a permanent set that could represent a whole variety of locations. In later centuries, painted and constructed scenery was provided for each particular production (see 4.2).

The modern designer has a variety of options open to him. He can set his production in-the-round (see 5.1), using a variety of rostra to form a symbolic setting or furniture to suggest a more realistic one. Alternatively he can design a setting on a more conventional stage and must then decide what kind of backdrop to select:
Bare stage – with the help of lighting, this concentrates all the attention on the actors, and costumes and properties.

Curtain set – an empty stage but one dressed with a background of curtains. These should be dark in colour to allow the actors to stand out against them. It is possible to add arches, pillars, etc. which will stand out against this type of backdrop and so give depth and interest to the setting.
Painted backcloth – particularly suitable for non-realistic productions such as pantomime.
Box-set – with the use of flats, three 'walls' are constructed to form a realistic room on stage. The audience looks in through the fourth 'wall'.
Cyclorama – a plain white wall which can be flood-lit in a variety of colours. This is particularly useful for open-air scenes. Free standing scenery and furniture can be placed in front of the cyclorama.
Many of these can be combined to good effect.

Frequently only certain types of setting will be possible on a particular stage, but ideally the type of setting should be dictated by the play. It is the designer's job to decide which type of backdrop will be most effective.

The Roman theatre at Sabratha, Libya

1.12   Costume: planning

A well–designed costume draws attention to the actor – not to the costume. It helps him to stand out against scenery and can even make him appear taller or thinner or fatter than he really is. It will help the audience to identify him and will indicate the character of the role he is playing. Changes in character during the play can be indicated by changes of costume. For example, a very formal character who gradually 'thaws' during the play can be dressed in formal clothes in the first scenes but in more casual wear in later ones.

Whoever is responsible for designing or planning the costumes for a production should go through the following steps:
1.   Read the script and discover the style and mood of the play.
2.   Now study the script and list the number of costumes needed for each character.
3.   Discuss with the director, or designer, what he wants the various costumes to suggest about each character, for example mood and status.

Discuss the range of colours that will be involved – what colours will be reserved for particular groups of characters?

4.   Discover what sort of stage the production is to take place on. How close will the audience be to the actors?

5.   Build up a detailed costume plot – listing the characters one by one, and filling in all the items of clothing they will need, scene by scene.

6.   Take the measurements – height, waist, shoe size, etc. of each member of the cast.

7.   Decide which items you have available, which must be borrowed or hired and which must be made.

8.   Decide when fittings will take place.

9.   Remember that the more an actor can rehearse in his costume, the more 'at home' in it he will become. Actors should never be 'surprised' by their costumes at final rehearsals.

Note that when working on classical plays, costumes can often be quite stylised. Look at the illustrations: how could these styles be adapted for use in dressing projects you have been working on or are about to start work on?

1.13   Lighting: spotlights

In the theatres of ancient Greece and in medieval and Shakespearean England, there was no stage lighting. Greek plays took place in the bright Mediterranean sunshine; English theatre had more variable lighting. By Victorian times, there was gas lighting in theatres. Now we have all the advantages of modern electric lamps or 'lanterns'.

There are four main purposes of stage lighting:

1.   to help the audience to see the actors clearly;

2.   to concentrate attention on a particular part of the stage;

3.   to create a particular atmosphere – evening, gloom, happiness or sunshine.

4.   to create special effects – strobe lighting, ultra-violet effects or projected images.

    The first need in stage lighting is to create a pool of light in which an actor can stand and be seen.

    The best lantern for this purpose is a Fresnel spotlight – Rank Strand Patt 833. In a spotlight,

there is a reflector, the light passes through a lens and then becomes a beam which can be focused. A Fresnel spot, with its ridged lens, produces a soft-edged pool of light. If you can use only one or two lanterns to light a stage, then use Fresnels. They should be placed FOH (front of house = in the auditorium), and high enough not to cast shadows on the back wall of the stage.

    Experiment until they light the area required without spilling light outside the acting area or the proscenium arch. 'Barn doors' can be fitted to direct the light, and the lamps can be focused to widen or narrow the beam.

    A Profile spot, Rank Strand Electric Patt 23,

has a smooth lens and the beam shape and size are governed by four independently adjustable shutters. Thus it tends to be useful in lighting a precise area, or in picking out a particular 'spot'.

If you have three lanterns in use, place two Fresnels FOH, and use a Profile spot backstage – say from high in the wings, to give depth and interest to the lighting.

One problem with Fresnel lanterns is that a certain amount of light 'spills' where you don't want it. So once you are using four or more lanterns use the Fresnels behind the proscenium arch. Place the Profile spots FOH to light your actors, especially their faces, from the front, and the Fresnels above the front of the stage on a lighting bar and in the wings.

Unless you have a particular reason for adding light from one direction, for example 'sunlight' coming in through an open door, always balance your lighting with a lantern stage left for each one stage right so that your actors are not lit from only one side.

Experiment with your lighting until you can achieve an even area of light across the stage without your actors casting shadows and without light spilling into the audience. Check that there are no sudden patches of intense light and that there are no areas, for example a chair where an actor will be seated for some time, that are not properly lit.

1.14   Sound

For many years, electrically reproduced or amplified sound was taboo in the theatre. The actor and singer would never admit to needing a microphone in order to reach the gallery, and sound effects were created by ironmongery, wind machines, dried peas and assistant stage managers.

New styles of theatrical production in which sound can replace scenery, technical advances and the influence of pop have all made electronic sound an important element in the creative process we call theatre, and the professional 'sound designer' may expect a sound system that would not disgrace a broadcasting or recording studio. All of which, together with home hi-fi standards, means that a gramophone in the wings or a distorting public address system is

not good enough for a school hall cum theatre, or indeed any theatre.

The shape of the Greek theatre, built into the hillside, naturally amplified the actor's voice. This is not the case in more recent theatres, and particularly not in theatres with a proscenium arch, see diagram 1. It is in this type of theatre that the actor must project his voice with especial care (see 1.6).

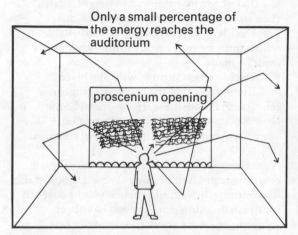

Diagram 1 – in theatres with a proscenium arch, much of the sound from the actors is blocked and therefore lost.

Microphones can be used to amplify the voice of an actor or singer, but unless radio microphones, which do not need wires and which can be clipped on to the actors' costumes, are available, this means the actor is restricted to staying near the microphone.

Certain points should be borne in mind about the positioning of loudspeakers, through which the audience will hear any amplified speech, recorded music, etc.:
1.   they should be as near the stage as possible so as to maintain the illusion of the sound coming from the actors or the set;
2.   they should be on the audience side of any microphones in order to lessen feedback;
3.   they should be angled to provide sound to every seat in the house.

A good position is directly above the stage. Remember: sound is like light. A person can sit under a spotlight beam and be lit by the general glow, while another person further away from the source can be fully lit. Therefore, tilt the

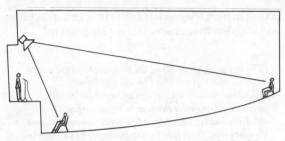

Diagram 2 – by aiming the loudspeaker at the back of the auditorium, an arc of sound is created encompassing the whole audience.

loudspeaker so that the maximum amount of sound is aimed at the rear of the auditorium – possibly at a point three rows down from the back, so as not to 'starve' the front rows of sound, see diagram 2.

When working on a production, remember all the various available sources of sound besides the natural voices of the actors:
 amplified voices, from the stage and off stage;
 recorded music;
 live music, (non-musicians should not be afraid of tackling percussion instruments!)
 spot effects (see 2.14);
 sound effects on discs.

Some technical terms:
amplifier – a device for magnifying electrical signals.
balance – the balance of loudness between various microphones or loudspeakers; also the balance between bass, middle and treble sounds.
channel – a complete sound or signal path, from source to outlet.
decibel (dB) – a measure of sound intensity.
distortion – any difference between the original sound and the recorded or reproduced sound.
dubbing – copying or duplicating sound on tape.
editing – process of cutting and re-arranging sections of recorded tape.
level indicator – indicates the level of a sound signal.
mixer – a device for mixing a number of signals, for example different effects or voice and music, in the required proportion.
P.A. – public address system.
playback – reproducing recorded sound.
splicing tape – non-magnetic tape used in editing.

1.15 Masks

As we have noted, actors in the Greek theatre wore masks (see 1.2). Masks have also been used in many other forms of theatre, as well as in tribal rituals. They can be used to suggest a whole range of expressions – some realistic, others highly exaggerated or even distorted.

Invent masks that will represent animals or people with particular temperaments – perhaps the different elements (see 1.8), or the four humours (see 2.5). Invent a ritual dance and design masks for the ritual.

Because the expression of a mask is fixed, emphasis is thrown on the body of an actor wearing one – movement must be carefully developed to match the appearance of the mask.

 When putting on a mask, sit or stand by yourself. Hold the mask in your hands. Stare at it. Imagine the character that will inhabit the mask. When you are ready, put it on slowly. Then stare at yourself in a mirror. Slowly, in movement, bring the creature or person to life. Then find ways of making sounds or speaking that match the expression and the movement.

Eye masks are the easiest to make. They can be made from card or felt or papier mâché. They can be painted or decorated with sequins or old ornaments. Felt ones must obviously be worn on elastic, others can either be worn this way or attached to a short length of dowel and held in the hand.

Half–face masks can suggest a whole variety of characters and creatures. They allow for clearer speech than *full–face masks* – but the latter of course can give a stronger visual image. Both kinds are made by moulding a clay or plasticine mould of the size and shape required and then by building up a papier mâché mask on the mould. Grease the mould to prevent sticking. Cut out eye and mouth holes before the mask dries.

1.16   Back-stage

In charge of all that happens 'back–stage' is the stage manager or 'SM'. His or her job is outlined in unit 5.16, but it should be stressed that his work begins long before the final rehearsals. He or his assistant 'stage manages' all rehearsals (that is sees that space is available, etc.) and works closely with the other departments during all the planning stages. For example, he will be involved in discussions between the director and designer, the director and lighting engineer, and also with those in charge of sound effects, etc.

His boss is the director; under him are those responsible for making properties (see 2.16), the carpenters (see 3.16 and 4.16), the costume department and also the assistant stage manager, his own immediate assistant (see 5.16).

1.17   Assessment

In practical drama work, it is sometimes difficult to assess whether progress is being made. When a play is actually produced in front of an audience, a clearer idea can be obtained. Sometimes that is too late! The following is an excerpt from a farce called *Streuth*. It sets out to make fun of a kind of detective thriller and also of bad amateur acting. Besides enjoying over-acting in it, discuss what faults in writing, acting and stage–management it is making fun of!

(The house lights are dim, the stage curtains are closed. Music: 'Mars' from The Planets by Holst.
Above the music the Cast can be heard getting into position, falling over the furniture, swearing, shushing, etc. Eventually, the Stage Manager remembers to raise the **curtain,** *revealing the* **Inspector**, **Mr and Mrs D'Arcy**, *the* **Major** *and* **Hubert** *grouped motionless around a settee and staring desperately at the audience. The* **Inspector** *prepares to speak, but is suddenly transfixed by the vacant area of stage in front of his feet. He quivers, blinks and looks nervously into the wings. The* **curtain** *comes down. 'Mars' resurfaces, comes to an end and is followed by a snatch of something totally inappropriate.)*
(The **curtain** *rises again. The vacant space at the* **Inspector's** *feet is now occupied by a dummy which has a huge poker protruding from its chest. If the corpse is a live actor, he should clasp the murder weapon.)*

Inspector   Now. Will you be good enough to identify the deceased, please.

D'Arcy (Peering at the corpse, registering shock)   My brother, actually. Henry.

Mrs D'Arcy (Over the top)   Poor, dear 'Enery. I just can't believe it!

D'Arcy   Really, Inspector, can't this interrogation wait. . . ?
(The actor who plays **D'Arcy** *regards his lines as something to be got rid of as soon as possible. The preceeding line should therefore be delivered as 'Really, Inspectorcan'tthisinterrogationwait?')*

Inspector (Taken back) Er . . .
(Recovering quickly)   Afraid not, sir. Perhaps you would be good enough to tell me where you all were when the murder was committed.

D'Arcy   Well, Inspector, Iwasinthedining-room,finishingoffapieceofCamembertwhenI heardthis – *(breath)* – screamaterriblescream followedbyadullthudIrushedoutintothehallandI happenedtonoticethatthegrandfatherclocksaid fivetonine. . . .

Mrs D'Arcy   Oh, no, Olivah, I was in the kitchen giving Cook the menu and the nine o'clock news was on the wireless.

Hubert   No . . . Mater . . . That . . . can't be right.
(He 'dries' and pulls out a cigarette case with the lines inside) . . . I was . . . in . . . the . . . library . . . reading . . . Buckle's History of Civilization . . . when . . . I . . . heard . . . a . . . scream . . . *(He dries again and changes to another cigarette case)* automatically . . . looked . . . at . . . my . . . wrist . . . watch . . . and . . . noticed . . . that . . . the . . . time . . . was . . . seven . . . thirty-five.

*(At this point, **Hubert** utilizes a traditional corny joke, by looking at his wristwatch and pouring the contents of his glass into **Mrs D'Arcy's** lap.)*

Inspector   Hmm – there seems to be a discrepancy here. This is most suspicious – I wonder what the explanation could be.

(A pause)

Major   Seems pretty obvious to me, Inspector, by Jove, by Jove!

Inspector   Does it, sir?

Major   Yes – er – ah! I would surmise that his wristwatch – *(he indicates **D'Arcy Senior**)* – and his grandfather clock – *(he indicates **D'Arcy Junior**)* – were both wrong.

Inspector   I believe, sir, you have hit upon the solution, sir. *(He goes to raise his hand, index finger pointing to the skies in an 'aha' position, only to find his hand is stuck in the lining of his raincoat. After a struggle, he manages to free it and strikes the pose)* And what were you doing while this was going on?

(A pause)

Major   Who, me?

Inspector *(Laughing nervously)*   Yes, sir. *You!*

Major *(He asks the next line as if it were a question)* I was taking a breath of fresh air in the garden, Inspector?

Inspector *(Sighing relievedly)*   I see, sir, did you hear the scream?

Major   No, Inspector, can't say I did, though I did see something deucedly funny.

Inspector *(With venom)*   Oh, and what was that?

Major   A figure, Inspector, at the drawing-room window, wearing evening dress.

Inspector   Was it the deceased, sir?

Major   No, Inspector, don't think it was. It was a broad-shouldered chappy with a long black beard.

Inspector   Could it have been either of these two gentlemen, here?

Major   It's so damned difficult to tell. The moment I caught sight of him, the damned light went off.

Inspector *(Raising his finger)*   That would imply there was someone else in the room at the time?

Major   By Jove, Inspector, you're right! By Jove!

*(The **Major**, having finished his lines at last, resumes his inane grin.)*

When watching practical work in rehearsal, get in the habit of judging whether the actors are really absorbed in their roles, whether they are working well as a group, whether the speech is clear and audible, whether the movement is easy and natural, whether space is being used well and the characterisation is convincing.

When working on a project, a group should keep on discussing the following points:

Shape – Does the programme have a beginning, middle and an end? Does it follow a logical progression?

Material – Is the material from a variety of sources? How well is the material arranged? Is it varied enough?

Multi-media – Is the group making the best use of lighting, sound effects, music, costume and scenery?

Co-operation – Is the group working well together on the presentation and co-operating with each other?

Conviction – Is the group sincere and convincing in its intentions and performance?

Individual's assessment – How well is each individual contributing to the planning of the presentation and its execution?

1.18   Project: Prometheus

This is one of the Greek myths about Prometheus who, it is said, created man from the dust of the earth – and then gave him many gifts.

Man as first created was little better than the beasts, a poor creature who knew little, ate raw meat and herbs and knew nothing of medicine.

But Prometheus taught men the arts and crafts of life. He taught them to build homes, and tools; to plough and sow, to reap and thresh, but it was slow work since Fire, the greatest aid, was missing. Without it meat must still be eaten raw and tools could be made only of stone; bread could not be baked and a house could not be warmed in winter.

Now Zeus, the king of the gods, had decreed that man should never be given the use of fire, but, even so, Prometheus made his way to the summit of Olympus; where he needed but to touch the golden wheel of the sun-chariot with a branch of wood. And so with the precious spark ignited, he hastened down the mountain side till he came to a deep valley and there he heaped up a pile of wood and kindled it. Slowly and shyly men gathered round the clearing where Prometheus had lit the first camp fire and gradually they drew nearer, enjoying its warmth. And one was so delighted he tried to kiss the tallest and brightest flame, but as it scorched him he drew back hastily, to the amusement of Prometheus. But more serious work was in hand, and when day dawned, he began to teach man the

keep men in slavery had been stolen and given to them, summoned Prometheus before him.

'You have disobeyed me . . . what is to prevent me from casting you into the depths and destroying these vile insects, these men, to whom you have given gifts reserved for the Immortals alone?'

'Lord Zeus,' answered Prometheus, 'I know how cruelly you will punish me for all I have done. But you cannot take away the gift that an Immortal has once given, so you cannot now deprive man of fire.'

The wrath of Zeus was terrible. In a voice of thunder he bade Might and Strength take Prometheus and bind him with fetters of brass to a mountain on the eastern edge of the world. 'There you shall lie for ever as a punishment for your daring and your disobedience. The snows of winter shall freeze you and the summer sun will burn you. And a fierce eagle will visit you every day and devour your liver, and every night your liver will grow again so that next day your agonies may be repeated.' And so the two demons, Might and Strength, took Prometheus and chained him to the rock with fetters he could not break; and the eagle did as Zeus had said, and the screams of Prometheus echoed over the haunted cliffs and chasms, unheard by man . . .

uses of fire. He showed them how to cook meat and to bake bread; how to make bronze and to smelt iron; to make swords and ploughshares . . . And now that Fire had come on Earth, it could be kindled whenever it was needed.

But Zeus, once he knew that he had been disobeyed and the gift which he had withheld to

Improvise a script and then rehearse and stage a play about Prometheus. Among the characters you could include are Prometheus, Zeus, the demons Might and Strength, various humans (farmers, cooks and metal-workers), and a chorus as narrator and commentator. You may also be able to use ideas you have developed when working on earlier units in this section.

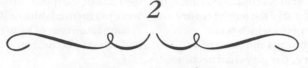

2
Medieval Theatre

2.1 Stages: rostra

The simplest of stages is an empty space. The next development is the introduction of various acting levels – as happened in the Greek theatre (see 1.2). Similar variety can be achieved in drama studios and on modern stages by the use of rostra.

By using rostrum blocks, space can be broken up into different levels. This changes the visual effect and adds interest to the setting. It alters the relationships between characters. Those standing on a higher level gain status while those on lower levels naturally appear to be more lowly. Corners between blocks can serve as hiding places and natural crevices, so by using blocks a varied landscape can be simulated. Ramps and steps are also useful. So too are triangular and segment-shaped blocks.

Collapsible rostra are of course easier to store but may not be as steady as more permanent blocks.

If you set out to make rostra, don't make them too small. They are of little use if there isn't room for a character or group of characters to stand comfortably on a particular level. Equally, don't fill up your acting area with so many blocks that movement becomes restricted.

Experiment by staging scenes on different levels. What effect do changed levels have on work? If blocks are not available, use tables, chairs and desks. How can the levels be best used in a particular scene?

A group of rostrum blocks can be put together to serve as one simple raised stage – like the kind medieval mystery plays were staged on.

2.2 Theatres: Medieval

Early medieval church services contained rituals
that were very like drama. By the tenth century
these had become short plays which were
mimed and chanted by monks and choirboys.
By the thirteenth century, the plays had become
very much more elaborate and also highly
popular. Quite a lot of comedy was gradually
introduced into the stories and they could no
longer be included in church services.
Consequently the church authorities decided to
transfer the plays to the church grounds, and
around this time the clergy ceased taking part in
the plays.

The organisation of the plays was taken over
by the trade 'guilds', and sequences of plays,
known as 'Mystery Cycles', were created. Each
guild acted a play suited to its profession, and the
play was performed on a mobile 'pageant
wagon' at various places in the town. After each
performance the cart was moved on to the next
stop and the play was presented once again. By
staying in one place an audience would see the
Bible story enacted in order, each scene being
performed on a different cart by a different guild.

So developed one of the first forms of 'street
theatre'. In most towns they were performed on
the feast of Corpus Christi, but in Chester they
were performed during Whit Week. One
account survives of how the plays were
performed in Chester.

They (the Chester pageants) were divided into
twenty-four pageants or parts, according to the
number of the Companies of the City, and every
Company brought forth their pageants, which was
the carriage or place which they played in.

They were played upon Monday, Tuesday and
Wednesday in Whitsun week. And they first began
at the Abbey gates, then it was wheeled from thence
to the Prentice at the High Cross before the Mayor;
and before that was done, the second came, and the
first went into the Watergate Street, and from
thence unto the Bridge Street, and so all, one after
another, till all the pageants were played appointed
for the first day, and so likewise for the second and
the third day. This pageant or carriage was a high
place made like a house with two rooms, being
open on the top; in the lower room they apparelled
and dressed themselves, and in the higher rooms
they played; and they stood upon six wheels.

David Rogers in the *Breviary of Chester History* 1609

Notice how the height of the pageant carts would allow the crowds in the street to have a clear view of the stage.

In recent times, some groups have presented medieval mystery plays on the backs of lorries. How else could they be presented? What locations in your area would be suitable for street theatre? What sort of plays would be likely to be well-received?

2.3   The Mystery Plays

As few of the members of the medieval guilds could read, there was not much point in making lots of copies of the scripts of the mystery plays.

However, there were scripts and several have survived. We possess copies of the plays that were performed in York, where there were forty-eight separate plays; Chester, twenty-four plays; and Wakefield, thirty-two plays. These last ones were also known as the Townely plays. Some of the plays performed at Coventry also survive.

As was explained in the last unit, several comic scenes not in the Bible were added to these plays. In the Wakefield Shepherds' Play, the three shepherds – Coll, Gib and Daw, are visited by a well-known scoundrel, Mak. Mak is intent on stealing a sheep and in the hope of not being recognised puts on a southern accent. NB Because this is a northern play, all the shepherds speak with strong northern accents.

(**Coll**, **Gib** and **Daw** *are sitting down, gazing at their sheep.* **Mak** *enters with a cloak over his tunic.*)

Mak *(aside)*   May they not know my will!
  (aloud)   Here's a man walks on the hill
    In search of peace.
Gib   Mak, where hast thou been? Tell us tidings.
Daw   Oh, has he come! Let each look to his things.
  (**Mak** *pretends not to know* **Coll**, **Gib** *and* **Daw** *and affects a southern accent*)
Mak   What! I am a yeoman, I tell you, of the king's.
    That from a great lord a great message brings.
Daw   It's a lie.
Mak   Fie on you! Go hence!
  (**Coll**, **Daw** *and* **Gib** *close in on* **Mak**)
Coll   Come, Mak, ye do wrong. Why speak ye so quaint?
Gib   I suppose that ye long to pass off as a saint.
Daw   How the rogue stands like a picture of paint!
Mak   I'll have you all bound. I'll make a complaint
    To my lord.
    Hands off, or ye'll hang!
Coll   Come drop that southern twang,
    Or ye'll get such a bang
    As a reward.
Mak   If you all three know me, I suppose I must
    believe you. You are fair company. I will not
    deceive you.
Gib   Ye're deep!
    Since so late you stray,
    What will good men say?
    For some think ye've a way
    Of stealing sheep.
Mak   Why, all men know I'm as true as steel,
    But I keep going hot and sickness I feel,
    And my belly fair aches – with pain I could
    squeal.
Coll *(yawning)*   Peace, Mak! Ye're not alone with an
    ache.
    I am utterly weary with staying awake;
    My limbs are exhausted; they tremble and shake,
    Keep watch, Gib, whilst I just a little nap take.
Gib *(yawning)*   Not I.
    For beside thee I'll creep;
    I too must have sleep.
    Daw, look to our sheep
    If they should cry.
  (He lies down)
Daw   I'm as good a man's son as any of you;
    So I'll lay myself down without more ado.
  (He lies down and seizes **Mak** *as he does so)*
    But Mak, come you here and lie twixt us two.
Mak *(pulling away)*   I've not said my prayers yet. I'll
    just say a few.
  (Kneeling to pray)   From my head unto my toe,
    Lord, be ever near! Amen.
  (**Coll**, **Gib** *and* **Daw** *are now apparently asleep*)

Mak *(sits up and speaks)*   Now were time for a man
    who is seeking a boon
    To seize a fat sheep and run off with it soon.
  (**Coll**, **Gib** *and* **Daw** *snore*)
Mak   How hard they sleep! That may ye all hear.
    I was never a shepherd, but I'll learn, never fear.
    If the flock be scared, I shall just nip near.
    Why, here comes something that right good
    cheer
    Will make.
    A fat sheep, I dare say!
    A good fleece, I dare lay!
    This one will I take.
  (**Mak** *seizes a sheep and goes off*)

Try devising your own 'modern mystery play'.
Think what comic characters and scenes you
could add – but remember, in the medieval plays
any comic scenes were kept separate from
serious ones which taught the main points of the
Bible story.

2.4   Improvisation: characterisation

One way of developing improvisation is to
work from character points. Below are
descriptions of four pilgrims from Chaucer's
Canterbury Tales (see 2.18):

THE SQUIRE (his father is the Knight)

He had his son with him, a fine young Squire,
A lover and cadet, a lad of fire
With locks as curly as if they had been pressed.
He was some twenty years of age, I guessed.
In stature he was of a moderate length,
With wonderful agility and strength.
He was embroidered like a meadow bright
And full of freshest flowers, red and white.
Singing he was, or fluting all the day;
He was as fresh as is the month of May.
Short was his gown, the sleeves were long and
wide;
He knew the way to sit a horse and ride.
He could make songs and poems and recite,
Knew how to joust and dance, to draw and write.
He loved so hotly that till dawn grew pale
He slept as little as a nightingale.

THE YEOMAN

This Yeoman wore a coat and hood of green,
And peacock-feathered arrows, bright and keen
And neatly sheathed, hung at his belt, the while

– For he could dress his gear in yeoman style.
His arrows never drooped their feathers low
And in his hand he bore a mighty bow.
His head was like a nut, his face was brown.
He knew the whole of woodcraft up and down.
A medal of St Christopher he wore
Of shining silver on his breast, and bore
A hunting-horn, well slung and burnished clean,
That dangled from a baldrick of bright green
He was a proper forester I guess.

THE NUN

There also was a Nun, a Prioress.
Her way of smiling very simple and coy.
Her greatest oath was only 'By St Loy!'
At meat her manners were well taught withal;
No morsel from her lips did she let fall,
Nor dipped her fingers in the sauce too deep;
But she could carry a morsel up and keep
The smallest drop from falling on her breast.
For courtliness she had a special zest.
And she would wipe her upper lip so clean
That not a trace of grease was to be seen
Upon the cup when she had drunk; to eat,
She reached a hand sedately for the meat.
She was so charitably solicitous
She used to weep if she but saw a mouse
Caught in a trap, if it were dead or bleeding.
And she had little dogs she would be feeding
With roasted flesh, or milk, or fine white bread
And bitterly she wept if one were dead
Or someone took a stick and made it smart;
She was all sentiment and tender heart.

THE MILLER

The Miller was a chap of sixteen stone,
A great stout fellow big in brawn and bone.
Broad, knotty and short-shouldered, he would
    boast
He could heave any door off hinge and post,
Or take a run and break it with his head.
His beard, like any sow or fox, was red
And broad as well, as though it were a spade;
And, at its very tip, his nose displayed
A wart on which there stood a tuft of hair
Red as the bristles in an old sow's ear.
His nostrils were as black as they were wide.
He had a sword and buckler at his side,
His mighty mouth was like a furnace door.
A wrangler and buffoon, he had a store
Of tavern stories, filthy in the main,
His was a master-hand at stealing grain.

By yourself, work out how these characters
might walk and talk. What mannerisms and
habits have they? What are their interests? What
might they think of each other?

See unit 2.18: what sort of person is the Wife
of Bath?

Improvise dialogues between different pairs of
pilgrims. Now work in larger groups. One of
you can be the host or 'compère'; the others
different pilgrims. Improvise a sort of medieval
version of a television chat show – it is the host's
job first of all to get the 'guests' to talk about
themselves, then to talk to each other.

Improvise a meal at which all five pilgrims are
present. Remember to keep in character.

2.5   Movement: the four humours

In medieval times, before the birth of modern
medicine, it was commonly believed that a
person's character was dependent on the balance
and mixture of four substances in the body:
    phlegm;
    choler;
    blood, called 'sangwyn';
    bile, called 'malencolye'.
The characteristics of these 'humours' are
indicated by the modern words derived from
them:
    phlegmatic – watery, sluggish, idle;
    choleric – angry;
    sanguine – courageous, hopeful;
    melancholic – sad, gloomy.
    Medieval medicine aimed to keep these
substances in the correct balance, but it was
realised that certain individuals possessed more
of one than the others. There was also thought to
be a connection between the humours and the
four ancient elements:

Melancholy (earth)

The melancholic hath nature of earth, cold and
dry. He is heavy, covetous, backbiter, malicious
and slow.

Phlegmatic (water)

The phlegmatic hath nature of water, cold and
moist. He is heavy, slow, sleepy, ingenious.

Choleric (fire)

The choleric hath nature of fire, hot and dry, naturally is lean and slender, covetous, ireful, hasty, brainless, foolish, malicious, deceitful and subtle were he applieth his wit.

Sanguine (air)

The sanguine hath nature of air, hot and moist. He is large, plenteous, attempered, amiable, abundant in nature, merry, singing, laughing, liking, ruddy and gracious.

Work out ways of moving that express each of these humours. Try to show each of the characteristics connected with the particular humours. Remembering the work you did for unit 1.8, create in movement encounters between people of different humours.

Work in groups in which members 'coax' each other from showing the characteristics of one humour into a more 'balanced' state. NB After each exercise, discuss how your movements could be developed to become more varied and more expressive. Don't exaggerate them to the point where they become merely comic.

2.6 Speech: variation

When beginning to work on a script, some actors do not always realise just how many ways there are of saying a line. How do you think the speech 'Now what do I do?' is being said by the actor in each of the photographs below?

How many different meanings can you give the line?

Now work on these separate lines:
'I've just given up smoking.'
'I always use a deodorant.'
'I want to be alone.'
'Excuse me, was there something?'
'Very well then, I shall join the Navy!'
'I'm all right now.'
Practise saying each of them in some of the following ways:

aristocratic	very humble	fearful
bored	sympathetic	angry
nervous	amazed	proud
tearful	loving	shy

Now select one *suitable* way of saying each line. Working in small groups, see if the rest of your group recognises the interpretation you are trying to give in each line.

In pairs, rehearse this short scene as if it is part of a popular comedy show on television. You hope the audience will find the situation funny.

(**Mavis** is sitting down; **Fred** enters)

Mavis   Oh, there you are, Fred. I thought you was never coming. Where shall we go? There's a good film on at the Odeon.
Fred   I ain't going to no film.
Mavis   Why ever not?
Fred (Pause)   I got the sack.

Mavis   What?... What for?
Fred   Stealing.
Mavis   Oh, Fred!

Now work on the scene as though it comes from a serious play. Play it first so that the audience sympathises with Mavis; then so that they sympathise with Fred.

In threes, work next on this scene. Play it first so that it has a happy ending, and then so it ends tragically or sadly.

(**Mother** sits in chair. **Sally** sits at her feet)

Sally   Well, I shall be glad when it's settled one way or the other.
Mother   Aye, it's worrying not hearing anything. (Pause) Well, Sally, it's getting late. We'd best be going to bed. (Knock)
Sally   Who can it be at this time of night?
Mother (Goes to door and unlocks it)   My boy! My son!
Son   I've come back, Mother. It's all over.

Now see how many different ways you can find of playing this scene. Which is most suitable?

B   Then you won't tell me where you were last night?
A   No.
B   I suggest you tell me.
A   I refuse. Absolutely.
B   Very well, then; there is no more to be said. But I warn you, you have not heard the last of this – by any means. (Exit)

NB In this unit, you have been working on short scenes out of context. Remember that when you come to work on longer scenes or on a whole play, it is not enough just to find out how many ways there are of playing a scene but is a matter of deciding which is the most suitable.

2.7 Acting: characterisation

'We usually start each rehearsal period with some warm-up exercises, and then with improvisations on character. The director selects characters which may seem to have nothing to do with the play at first, but when we discuss them afterwards, we see the various connections. This way we begin to discover what it's like to be a particular type of character and we compare our discoveries with the text. Which aspects of the characters we've invented match the character in the play, for example.'

So one actor describes a way of working from improvisation towards an understanding of character in a play. Usually this means improvising in roles gradually approaching those in the play.
'Walk like a very old man.'
'Now walk like an old man.'
'Now walk like a fit fifty year old.'
'Now walk like yourself.'
'Try the fit fifty year old again.'
'The same again, but this time he's humming a little tune to himself.'

And so on. Now try to invent a series of exercises that will help you to bring to life the character in the photograph. Once you have developed her walk, try to develop a way of talking that would reveal her character without being comic. What are her thoughts? Her fears and anxieties?

The good director will give his actors the chance to build the characters they are going to play, through experiment and discussion. 'That character you've just created – which points would suit the character in the play? Which details wouldn't be right?'

Here are three games that are helpful for exploring and understanding character:

This is your life

Those taking part need some time to prepare for this one. The 'life' will be that of the central character in the play, the rest of the cast take the parts they will have in the play, and the director can indulge himself as Eamonn Andrews. Brave groups may tackle it without preparation once they have begun to get to know the play. It is also useful for working out the relationships between characters.
Remember: each 'guest' will need a quotation to speak from off stage, when Eamonn Andrews says, 'And now do you recognise this voice?'

The moral trial

A 'tribunal' sits in judgement on a central character – was he or she justified in behaving as he or she did? Minor characters can be called as witnesses. This is a good way of increasing awareness of the whole play in each actor's mind, and it helps those involved to understand how each character reacts to the others.

The chat show

If 'the moral trial' is a particularly good way of understanding character and relationships in a tragedy – where a 'fault' in character, like jealousy or ruthless ambition, is being explored – staging a television chat show allows for improvisation in character of a more light-hearted nature (see 2.4).

38

2.8 Dance 1

With a partner, mime a tennis match. If necessary, slow the motions down a little and don't forget to keep your eye on the 'ball'. Add a percussion accompaniment to the mime.

Now rehearse the movements of other sports, perhaps in slow motion, and develop these into a dance of the different sports. Imagine it as a film sequence which might introduce a sports programme on television – it could be danced to the signature tune of such a programme.

Any movement with rhythm and form becomes dance. There are no basic rules – dance is simply movement through space.

Different systems have grown up in different countries and different ages. Music is not necessary but when it is used, it imposes a particular pattern on the movement. Develop your own dance to percussion rhythms.

Think of the various kinds of dance – classical ballet, disco, rock, African, ballroom, Scottish, Greek, Spanish, old-time, etc. Experiment in devising your own versions of these different styles of dancing. If anyone in your group knows about country dancing, morris dancing or sword dancing, you could include it in a project on medieval England.

39

2.9 The director

The director has many jobs. It is his job to: interpret the script, to see that what happens on stage reflects the author's intentions; understand the play – its plot, structure, characterisation, background and themes; visualise the play; select, guide, encourage and help the actors; link the work of the designer, the lighting engineer and those in charge of sound, music, costume and stage–management; keep within the budget set by the producer; provide the audience with as high a standard of entertainment as possible; to see that the company is not merely indulging itself; see that everything keeps to schedule, and that individual rehearsals start promptly.

So the director is responsible to:
the author;
the audience;
and, with the producer, must co–ordinate the work of all those involved in a production.

2.10 Staging the Guild Plays

The following is an excerpt from *Mrs Noah's Missing*, a musical comedy by David Self and Robert Long, which describes the attempts of the Guild of Water Carriers in medieval Chester to stage their play about Noah:

Elizabeth   Are we going to do the same play this year?
Alison   The one about Noah?
Will   The Water Carriers always do the play about Noah.
Nick   That's right. The play called 'Noah's Flood'.
Alison   Who'll play each part, Nick?
Ralph   Ned must be Mrs Noah.
Ned   Oh no. Oh no, no, no, no.
Nick   Yes, I think so. Ned can be Mrs Noah.
Ned   Oh no, I'm not going to play the part of Mrs Noah.
Nick   The thing is, we've got to get the pageant wagon ready.

Ralph I wondered why it had been standing here.

Nick It's got to be tidied up.

Hannah All the curtains and coverings need renewing.

Alison We'd better start work then.

Elizabeth What shall I do?

Nick You'll need needle and thread – all the tapestries want repairing.

Hannah They're in our house – you'll find them in the chest in the back room.

Ralph I'll start repainting it.

Elizabeth It'll look just like the Ark.

Ralph It will do when it's finished.

Will It's not as good as the one we had when I was young.

Hannah Go on with you, Will. You say that every year.

Will Well, it's true.

Ned I'm not going to have to wear a dress, am I?

Alison Don't worry. You'll look lovely.

Nick Ralph, here's a farthing; I want you to pop down to the chandler's and buy some grease.

(Gives him coin)

Launcelot Grease?

Nick Yes, to oil the wheels of the wagon. We don't want it squeaking round Chester like I don't know what.

Try improvising and developing your own play about a guild preparing to stage a mystery play. Or you could stage a documentary which explains how the plays developed from church rituals, moved into the open air and were staged on pageant carts. You could perhaps include the above scene and excerpts from actual mystery plays and show how they related to the Bible. You could also research other facts about the staging of the plays and about life in medieval England in general, and present this by means of dramatised scenes – linked by a narrator or ballad singer. You could also include scenes developed while working on unit 2.4.

2.11 Design: illustrating a text

It is the job of the designer to illustrate the background of a text, to provide the setting in which the action will take place. It is his job to select those details that will aid the actors and convey the writer's and the director's intentions to the audience. It is not his job to fill the stage with clutter or unnecessary distractions.

Some dramatists give a lot of instructions to designers. This is the opening direction of *The Caretaker* by Harold Pinter (see 5.5).

A room. A window in the back wall, the bottom half covered by a sack. An iron bed along the left wall. Above it a small cupboard, paint buckets, boxes containing nuts, screws, etc. More boxes, vases, by the side of the bed. A door, up right. To the right of the window, a mound: a kitchen sink, a step-ladder, a coal bucket, a lawn-mower, a shopping trolley, boxes, sideboard drawers. Under this mound an iron bed. In front of it a gas stove. On the gas stove a statue of Buddha. Down right, a fire-place. Around it a couple of suitcases, a rolled carpet, a blow-lamp, a wooden chair on its side, boxes, a number of ornaments, a clothes horse, a few short planks of wood, a small electric fire and a very old electric toaster. Below this a pile of old newspapers. Under **Aston**'s bed by the *left wall, is an electrolux, which is not seen till used. A bucket hangs from the ceiling.*

On the other hand, Samuel Beckett gives only this direction at the beginning of his play *Waiting for Godot:*

Act I
A country road. A tree. Evening.

This allows the designer to use his imagination but can cause problems. A famous designer, Timothy O'Brien, once sent some photos of a possible setting for the play to the author. By return post came this post card:

Dear Mr O'Brien,
Thanks for photos. All much too big and real. Faint tree upstage actor's left, faint stone downstage actor's right, faint path between, uninscribed sky and distance, evening light emptiness at all costs. For tree see text. Please don't start construction till I get over. Shall be in the theatre next Thursday morning.

Sincerely,
Samuel Beckett.

Do you prefer detailed instructions or ones that allow you to use your imagination?

When starting work on a design begin by studying the text. Attend first rehearsals and join in discussions with the director and cast,

A medieval interior

especially if it is a 'home-made' play or documentary. Discover what are the basic requirements of the play, for example the number and position of entrances and exits, any different levels and items of furniture that are required in the action.

Study reference books, paintings, costume books, architecture, photographs and slides of the period in question. Start making rough sketches of useful items that will provide a setting for the play and which might match the interpretation it is being given.

2.12 Making costumes

Design a set of simple costumes for a group of characters in a mystery play or a documentary about life in medieval England. Rely on tunics and tights or long stockings for the men; loose, simple dresses for the women. What is suggested by different colours? White? Black? Green? Red? What basic accessories can be usefully added? Belts? Neckerchiefs? Boots? How can you indicate the more important characters? Produce rough, coloured sketches and then, if possible, try making such costumes.

The costume designer must have some knowledge of dress–making and dyeing, etc. He or she should know where it is possible to get hold of cheap remnants of material; have the imagination to see how old costumes can be revived; and know where costumes can be borrowed or hired from.

Most of all, he or she must have an eye for line, shape, colour and texture. He or she must know where to find illustrations of period costumes, and how to select significant elements from such illustrations. After all, a costume must look right from the middle of the auditorium and that does not mean that every buttonhole and decoration need be correct in detail. Making stage costumes is easier than ordinary dress–making because it does not require the same degree of 'finish'. Try picturing costumes in silhouette. Outline is of supreme importance on stage.

Experiment with different materials. Which colours and textures combine naturally? What is meant by 'looking in period'? For example, why do some modern dressing gowns always look

like modern dressing gowns and never like colourful medieval cloaks?

Always work in conjunction with the lighting designer. What effect will different coloured light have on the costume colours you are planning? (See 4.13.) Remember, fabrics usually look better under lights of a similar colour.

2.13 Lighting: floodlights

Besides spotlights (see 1.13), the other main type of lantern is the floodlight. This is a much simpler lantern than the spotlight. It consists of a lamp and a reflector in a tin box which can be tilted up and down or panned from side to side. There is no other control; it cannot be focused, for example. It is not as *selective* as a spotlight, nor as powerful (because there is no lens).

Floodlights are generally used for lighting scenery; not for lighting acting areas. For example, they can be useful in 'killing' shadows made by actors.

A number of floodlights combined in one long unit is known as a *batten*. Usually these are wired in two, three or even four circuits so that different colour combinations can be used. When a batten sits on the front edge of the stage, it becomes known as the footlights. Battens are very useful for colour lighting a cyclorama back-ground or for lighting a backcloth.

Single floodlights can be used off stage behind windows and doorways.

A floodlight – generally used for lighting scenery.

2.14 Sound effects

Sound effects may be used:
1. to establish the locality; for example, sounds of the sea or city traffic;
2. to establish the weather; for example, wind or rain;
3. to establish the time of day; for example, owls;
4. to add atmosphere;
5. to indicate events off stage; for example, cars arriving, phones ringing, clocks striking;
6. to stimulate events on stage; for example, clocks chiming, babies crying.

Background effects should be used to establish scenes and then used sparingly. Fade them *very* gradually otherwise the audience will believe the rain has stopped, the sea disappeared, etc. Allow them to return from time to time.

Sound effect discs are the most convenient way of creating background effects. Various commercial ones are available from record shops. It is worth transferring such effects to tape, particularly if cueing the records is likely to prove difficult or if a production is going to have several performances. Coloured leader tape can be edited into the tape so that each effect can be easily located (see 5.14). This method will also allow you to lengthen any effect which does not last long enough on the disc – record the effect on tape twice and then edit together the two bursts of sound. Other sounds which have to be recorded ones, for example motor cars, can be included on this tape. Always check you know at what 'level' each sound must be played.

Certain sounds will always be more convincing if they are produced 'live'. Door and 'phone bells, door knockers, door slams and glass crashes are always more effective as live spot effects rather than using tape or disc substitutes. NB Glass should be broken into a box.

Other useful 'backstage effects' include:

a gravel tray, for footsteps;
a thunder sheet, sheet of galvanised iron;
dried peas or lead shot on a drum, for rain.

Sometimes it will be necessary to record your own effects. A good quality tape-recorder is

A sound effects cupboard

4. fire (crush cellophane paper close to the microphone);
5. footsteps in the snow (crunch a bag of flour close to the microphone);
6. footsteps in the forest (crunch a handful of old, unwound recording tape near the microphone).

2.15   Make–up: young characters

Theatrical make-up is used:

to emphasise the natural features of the face and to make them more distinctive in strong stage light;

to highlight the eyes;

to change or disguise appearance.

Make-up should be applied in strong light but away from any glare: not in a dingy backstage area. Neon lighting is especially good. A desk lamp shining onto the mirror can also provide good illumination.

Leichner Limited are the most famous manufacturers of stage make-up and their products can be recommended. Greasepaint is available in sticks, tubes and liners. Pan-Cake and Pan-stik are other forms of stage make-up but these are more expensive than traditional greasepaint.

For normal use, the following sticks or tubes will be required:

$4\frac{1}{2}$ Brownish tan;
5   Ivory;
8   Golden tan;
9   Brick red.

You will also need the following liners:

Black, Medium Brown, Dark Brown, Crimson Lake, Carmine 2.

Other necessary equipment includes:

powder, powder puff, tissues, removing cream, orange sticks, a fine paint brush, liquid make-up for limbs and body. The colours are numbered to match greasepaint sticks.

Preparation

Pin your hair out of the way, wash hands and face. If you have a dry skin, smear with removing cream and then wipe smooth with a tissue.

necessary for this. It is also vital that there should be no other noise around!

Experiment by trying to record the following sounds:

1. particular vehicles approaching and stopping;
2. particular vehicles starting up and moving off;
3. water lapping (agitate water in a plastic bucket and record in close up);

45

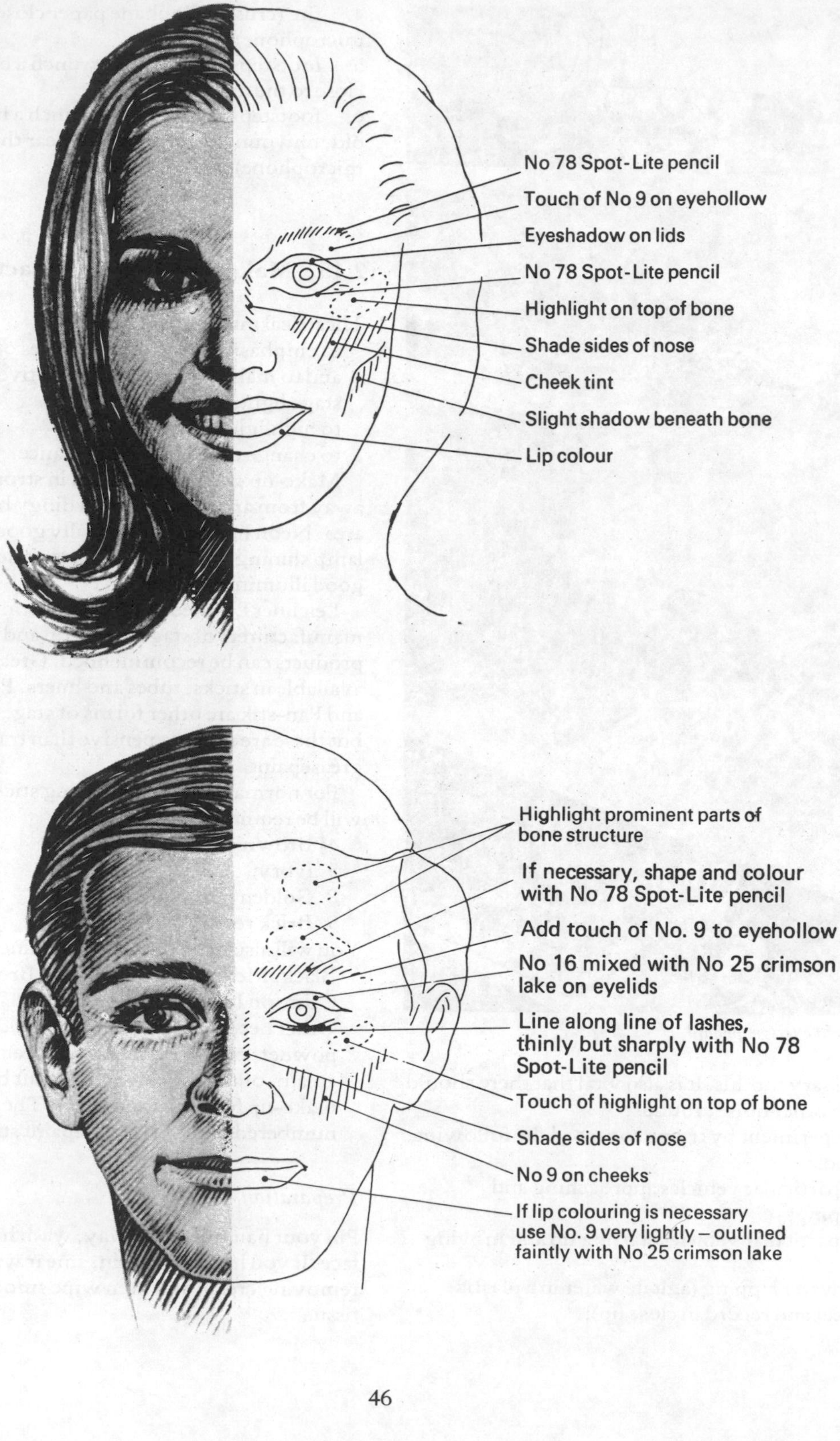

No 78 Spot-Lite pencil

Touch of No 9 on eyehollow

Eyeshadow on lids

No 78 Spot-Lite pencil

Highlight on top of bone

Shade sides of nose

Cheek tint

Slight shadow beneath bone

Lip colour

Highlight prominent parts of bone structure

If necessary, shape and colour with No 78 Spot-Lite pencil

Add touch of No. 9 to eyehollow

No 16 mixed with No 25 crimson lake on eyelids

Line along line of lashes, thinly but sharply with No 78 Spot-Lite pencil

Touch of highlight on top of bone

Shade sides of nose

No 9 on cheeks

If lip colouring is necessary use No. 9 very lightly – outlined faintly with No 25 crimson lake

Apply foundation colours – young men: 5 and 8, 5 and 9 if they are to look particularly healthy; young women: 5 and 4½. Blend together on the face until the correct shade is achieved. Cover the whole face – up to the hair-line and under the chin.

Add highlights to the cheeks, etc. if thought necessary. Apply as shown in the diagrams. To avoid leaving a hard edge use your fingers to blend the edges of the highlight areas with the rest of the face.

Now tackle the eyes – as shown in the charts. Emphasise the natural lines, don't exaggerate too much. Don't apply the liners directly. Daub a little onto your hand, then use an orange stick or fine paint brush to apply the make-up.

Lips: women may use a little Carmine 2; men 8 or 9.

Once the make-up is complete, dab on powder with a powder puff. Excess powder can be removed with a soft clean brush or a clean powder puff.

Don't forget to use liquid body make-up on hands and any other exposed parts of the body.

Note: the smaller the theatre, the less make-up you need. Don't overdo it. Do practise. Look at the results of your experiment under stage lighting. Practise until you can achieve a completely natural look, but one that concentrates attention on the actor – so that he or she looks 'right'. NB The charts give very full details of fairly elaborate make-up: experiment until you appreciate the effect of each detail from the audience's viewpoint.

2.16 Properties

There are three types of properties or 'props':
1. small articles which must be set on stage before the play begins, as opposed to larger items of furniture or scenery;
2. hand-props – articles, such as letters or coins, which belong to a particular character and are taken on stage by him;
3. costume props, such as purses or glasses, which are worn by an actor.

The person in charge of props is called either the property master (or mistress) or prop boy (or

girl), and is responsible to the stage manager. During the rehearsal period, it is his or her responsibility to find or make all the props required in a production, and to make a detailed list of them.

Before and during each performance, he or she must check that each prop is in place, receive any props carried off stage by the actors, and re-check them *all* against the list after each performance to make sure none are lost or need repairing. He or she is also responsible for replacing any props, such as food or drink, which are consumed on stage during a performance.

2.17   The producer

Nowadays, we usually use the word *director* to mean the person who directs the play, who is in charge of all that happens on stage. The *producer* is in charge of the business side. It is his job to see that all goes smoothly; he should know what needs doing when and by whom – and see that it gets done on time. He needs to be very tactful and also a good businessman.

He should take all the management problems off the director's shoulders so that the director can concentrate on the artistic side of the play. The producer is in charge of:

the publicity manager (see 4.17);
the box-office (see 5.17);
the house manager (see 5.17).

He is also in charge of finance of the production, the budget. He must know how much money is available for a production and decide, with the director and designer, how it should be used. He should also be aware of how he can raise extra money – for example by having advertising in the programme. The expenses of a production will vary but these are some of the areas where money will have to be spent:

Performing rights – normally these will have to be paid on all plays unless the author has been dead for more than fifty years.
Texts – hire or purchase of copies, or duplication of locally written scripts. Usually you need at least five copies beside the cast's – director, stage manager, lighting, prompter, sound.
Printing – posters; tickets; handbills; programmes.

Wardrobe – costume-hire; costumes to be made; items purchased; cleaning; sundry expenses.
Make-up and hairdressing – make-up, re-stocking; make-up, special purchases; haircutting and dressing; wigs.
Settings – materials, wood, hardboard, etc; ironmongery and fittings; paint and size; stage management, sundries.
Properties – property hire, including weapons; furniture hire; curtains and drapes; properties bought; materials for making properties.
Lighting, sound and effects – hire of additional lighting; special lighting effects; hire of sound equipment; purchase of tapes and records; sundry expenses, wiring, plugs, etc.
Transport – collection and return of hired goods by British Rail, BRS or private transport.
Administration, 'phone and postage.
Rent of hall, if applicable.

NB Refreshments are better run as a separate account and not included in the main budget.

The best way of understanding the job of a producer is to be the producer of an actual show. Improvising, planning and budget meetings can give you some practice.

2.18   Project: The Wife of Bath's Tale

Chaucer's *The Canterbury Tales* was written between 1386 and 1389. One long poem, it tells how a group of imaginary, but typical, pilgrims meet at the Tabard Inn in London and travel together to Canterbury to worship at the shrine of Thomas à Becket. On their way, the pilgrims keep each other entertained by telling stories.

One of them, the Wife of Bath is quite a character. When BBC Television dramatised *The Canterbury Tales*, the actress Barbara Jefford, who played the role, described her as 'sexy, shrewd and very, very prosperous . . . she's over forty which in the Middle Ages was the equivalent of sixty now, yet she's full of beans'. Chaucer tells us the Wife of Bath was somewhat deaf, had had five husbands, 'apart from other company', was bold and merry and wore bright red stockings.

Her story is set in the time of King Arthur. It concerns a lusty young knight who is condemned to death for raping a young maiden.

King Arthur sentences the knight to be executed and this is about to take place when Queen Guinevere and the other ladies of the court, perhaps somewhat taken with the handsome young knight, plead that his life may be spared. The king gives Guinevere the task of deciding what will happen to the knight. She tells him he may avoid the axe if, within the course of a year, he can find the answer to the question, 'What is the thing that women most desire?'

He agrees to try and sets off on his travels. He is given many possible answers: wealth, honour, gorgeous clothes, 'to be oft widowed and remarried', 'freedom to do as she pleases', and so on. But he finds no agreement. Saddened, he makes his way back to face his punishment as the year comes to an end.

On his way back, he meets a horrible old witch who asks him what's the matter. He tells her his story and she says she will give him the answer, guaranteeing it will be the one the queen wants; provided that in return he will do what she requests. He agrees, she whispers the answer in his ear, and he goes to the palace. All assemble to hear what he has to say. He gives the answer – a woman wants to be lord of her husband, she wants 'sovereignty' over him.

All those women present agree he is correct: 'He's saved his life!' they cheer.

Then the old witch enters, explaining she taught him the answer and claiming in return that the knight should marry her. He admits the truth of what she says and reluctantly agrees to the marriage.

On their wedding night, he is very gloomy. The witch asks him why – he tells her how ugly he finds her. She gives him two choices: to have her old, ugly and faithful; or young, beautiful and not-so-faithful. He thinks long about the matter and then says he will leave it to her to decide. She commands him to kiss her. He does – and his wife is transformed into a beautiful young girl. They live happily ever after, and the Wife of Bath concludes with a prayer that women may be sent husbands who are 'meek and young and fresh in bed'.

Improvise or script and then stage a play based on the story. In the early stages of your planning you will have to decide whether or not you will include the Wife of Bath herself as a storyteller, and how many other characters you will include. Decide too on what form of stage you could best present your play.

3

Shakespearean Theatre

3.1 Stages: thrust or apron

We have seen something of what medieval stages were like (see 2.2, 2.3 and 2.10): basically they were simply raised platforms.

As the guild plays declined and professional touring companies developed, new forms of theatre became necessary. Frequently these wandering actors would perform in an inn yard. A platform would be put up at one end of the yard so that the performers could be seen above the heads of the crowd, and any convenient door or window could be incorporated in the action. Ordinary people would watch from the inn yard; the rich would watch from the windows and galleries that looked out into the yard.

In 1576 the first building designed especially for the performance of plays was erected in London for a man called James Burbage. It was a wooden circular building and open to the weather. It copied many of the features of an inn yard; there were galleries around it from where the rich could watch the plays, and the stage thrust out from one wall into the middle of the area where ordinary people stood. This building was called 'The Theatre'.

This kind of thrust stage is of course surrounded by the audience on three sides. The great advantage of this is that the actors are not separated from the audience – they are there in the midst of them, rather like acting in-the-round. It is easy for an actor to make an 'aside' directly to the audience; and soliloquies can be spoken naturally, as though the speaker is sharing his thoughts with those around him.

On a proscenium stage, an actor must project such a speech – like any other – through the arch and out into the auditorium. This can frequently seem forced and 'stagey'.

But the thrust stage has a great advantage over acting in-the-round. There is a back wall which can serve as a castle, house, palace, town or whatever you wish. In Elizabethan times, it was one permanent set. In modern theatre, scenery for particular plays can be designed and installed. Because a thrust stage combines all the advantages of a theatre in-the-round – intimacy and immediacy, with those of a proscenium stage – scenery; it is not surprising that in recent years many theatres have been adapted to include a thrust, or apron, stage, and that new ones have been built to this plan.

In many traditional school and college halls, it may be possible to build a thrust stage out of large rostrum blocks on the front of a proscenium stage. For this to be really effective, the building must be wide enough to accommodate spectators on all three sides of the thrust stage. Alternatively, it may be possible to build a small apron stage which will at least allow the actors to come out of the proscenium arch a little way.

What similarities are there between a thrust stage and a Greek theatre? What is the one great difference?

3.2 Theatres: Shakespearean

The Globe, like most of the other theatres of Shakespeare's time, was about three storeys high and no more than 100 feet in diameter. Two thousand people crammed into this building to watch a play.

Inside, most of the theatres had the same plan. There would be a thrust stage jutting out into the middle of the audience. It is thought that this was probably forty feet wide, nearly thirty feet deep and perhaps four or five feet high. There are very few modern stages with such a large acting area.

There were two doorways at the back of the stage, one on either side, through which the actors made their entrances and exits. Note that it would take a few seconds for an actor to reach the front of the stage from one of these doorways. If you study a Shakespeare play you will see that characters quite often say lines like,

THE GLOBE THEATRE IN THE DAYS OF SHAKESPEARE. GEORGE PYCROFT DEL.

'Look, here comes . . . ' In the Elizabethan theatre such remarks sounded quite natural as the actor approached; on a modern stage they present difficulties because as soon as actors enter from the wings, they are immediately involved in the action.

At the back of the stage was the inner stage. This could be closed from view by drawing curtains across it. It could be used to represent inner rooms, caves and hiding places. Above this inner stage was a balcony or upper stage. This could represent an upstairs storey – remember the balcony scene in *Romeo and Juliet*; the walls of a castle – as at Harfleur in *Henry V* or in Act V of *Macbeth*; or simply a platform from which one character could address others – as Brutus and Antony do in *Julius Caesar*, Act III.

A canopy, supported by stage posts, covered much of the stage, but not the audience. High above the stage was a turret from which a trumpeter announced the start of each performance. There was also a musicians' gallery.

Spectators paid one penny to stand in the yard to view the play. They were nicknamed 'groundlings', because they stood on the ground. Better-off spectators paid twopence for admission to one of the galleries that surrounded the yard, while threepence could pay for admission to one of the galleries that had the best view of the stage. The very rich might pay even more for a seat on the stage itself (see 3.4).

There was little or no scenery. Simple properties or garments were sufficient, together with the lines, to indicate where the action was taking place. If a chair or stool were brought on stage, that told the audience the scene was indoors. If a character entered wearing riding boots, he had obviously just been travelling. A watchman carrying a lantern indicated it was night-time. Remember, the plays were acted in daylight; at this time there was no artificial stage lighting.

If you are studying a particular Shakespeare play in detail, work out which scenes you think might have taken place on the main stage, which in the inner stage, and which on the upper stage. Can you find any lines that would help an actor to make his entrance or exit, or move from one part of the stage to another?

3.3 Shakespeare

William Shakespeare was born in Stratford–
upon-Avon in 1564. His parents were quite
well-to-do; his father was a glover. Shakespeare
was educated at the local grammar school and in
1582 married Anne Hathaway. He left Stratford
about 1585.

He was next heard of in London where Lord
Southampton became his patron. By 1592 he
was established as a playwright and an actor,
becoming a member of the Lord Chamberlain's
group of actors (see 3.7).

By 1597 he was sufficiently rich to buy the
second largest house in Stratford, and the next
year he became a partner in the new Globe
Theatre. His earliest plays date from 1590. He
stopped writing about 1611 and retired to
Stratford where he died in 1616 and was buried
in the church there.

It is not possible to date his plays exactly, but the
following table gives some idea of the order in
which they were written:

	Comedies	Tragedies	Histories
1590			Henry VI (3 parts)
	Two Gentlemen of Verona		
	Comedy of Errors		
	The Taming of the Shrew		
			Richard III
		Titus Andronicus	
	Love's Labour's Lost		
		Romeo and Juliet	
1595	Midsummer Night's Dream		
			Richard II
			King John
	Merchant of Venice		
			Henry IV (2 parts)
			Henry V
	Much Ado About Nothing		
	Merry Wives of Windsor		
	As You Like It		

1600		Julius Caesar
		Troilus and Cressida
		Hamlet
	Twelfth Night	
	Measure for Measure	
	All's Well that Ends Well	
		Othello
		King Lear
		Macbeth
		Timon of Athens
		Antony and Cleopatra
		Coriolanus
1608	Pericles	
	Cymbeline	
	The Winter's Tale	
1611	The Tempest	
		Henry VIII

3.4 Improvisation: situations

We know that some of the actors in Shakespeare's company occasionally improvised in the course of a play. In particular those playing the comic roles seem to have added their own lines. Shakespeare does not appear to have approved. In a scene in *Hamlet*, Hamlet gives some advice to a group of wandering players who are about to perform a play:

Hamlet Let those that play your clowns speak no more than is set down for them, for there be of them that will themselves laugh, to set on some quantity of barren spectators to laugh too, though in the mean time some necessary question of the play be then to be considered. That's villainous, and shows a most pitiful ambition in the fool that uses it.

A play called *The Knight of the Burning Pestle* is about a group of actors who are set on performing a love story – when they are forced to improvise another kind of play.

The Knight of the Burning Pestle was probably written by Francis Beaumont in 1607 or 1608 for performance in the Blackfriars Theatre in London. This was a private theatre where plays were presented indoors by boy actors to an audience smaller than that of the public theatres and where the price for admission was correspondingly higher. The very rich would demand seats on the actual stage, from where they would often heckle the young actors.

The main plot of this play concerns Jasper, a poor apprentice in love with his rich employer's daughter. This rich merchant, Venturewell, is determined, however, that his daughter, the very lovely Luce, shall marry the more respectable but rather 'wet' Humphrey. So Jasper and Luce decide to elope . . .

But as the actors are beginning their performance, a grocer and his wife in the audience are upset. Would not an exciting story of a knight errant be more enjoyable than a love story? And why should their apprentice Rafe not have a part in the play? Rafe therefore becomes a grocer errant, with his trade's emblem, a pestle, emblazoned on his shield. It is up to the other actors to accommodate this extra character and his adventure, as best they can, within their play; and they must also cope with the interruptions of the grocer and his wife who insist on sitting on stage, and commenting on the action.

In groups, improvise and rehearse the story of Jasper. Then play these scenes to the other groups – but from the 'audience' come three 'interruptors', like the grocer and his wife, who insist that one of their number, perhaps a rather bashful character, has a part in the play.

In Beaumont's play, the grocer and his wife insist the actors include a variety of scenes from different types of entertainment then popular – such as romantic melodrama and even maypole dancing. In a modern version, these could be updated to become a pop star's act – mimed to a record, a television commercial or a popular television show.

The interruptions must not become too frequent, and it will be helpful if those playing the 'interruptors' appear to believe the basic plot is 'real', and if the actors remain polite to these very rich members of their audience!

Now develop an improvisation based on the situation in the cartoon.

This kind of improvisation requires discipline and care, but will be very helpful in developing confidence and fluency on stage. From it can develop many excellent entertainments – but while it is fair to make a new play in this way, remember Hamlet's advice if you are acting someone else's lines!

3.5 Movement: stage exercises

Movements on stage, particularly in costume plays, cannot be 'simply' realistic. In real life, our movements are often fussy, jerky or unnecessary. Movement on stage must be graceful and easy.

Practise walking – slightly slower than usual – and let your legs move from the hips, not the knees. Allow your hands to brush your hips, gently. Practise turning, slowly. Always lead off on the foot that's nearest the direction you're going. Don't swing round clumsily on one foot. Practise sitting down with dignity. Don't look round at the chair – secretly feel for it with your leg, then lower yourself into it. Practise going down on one knee, slowly. On stage, always kneel on the downstage knee. Why?

Now mime a variety of everyday actions – but ration your movements. Cut out unnecessary ones, and don't be afraid to hold a position – not tensely, but in a state of rest.

Keeping these points in mind, in pairs work on this scene. It is the opening of the play *Rosencrantz and Guildenstern Are Dead* (see 3.7). Don't add moves to the script – rely on the ones the author has written into the stage directions.

Two Elizabethans passing the time in a place without much visible character. They are well-dressed. Each of them has a leather money bag. **Guildenstern's** *bag is nearly empty.* **Rosencrantz's** *bag is nearly full. The reason being they are betting on the toss of a coin, in the following manner:* **Guildenstern** *takes a coin out of his bag, spins it.* **Rosencrantz** *catches it, studies it, announces it as 'heads' (as it happens) and puts it into his own bag. Then they repeat the process. They have apparently been doing this for some time. The run of 'heads' is impossible, yet* **Rosencrantz** *betrays no surprise at all – he feels none. However, he is nice enough to feel a little embarrassed at taking so much money off his friend. Let that be his character note.* **Guildenstern** *is well alive to the oddity of it. He is not worried about the money, but he is worried by the implications; aware but not going to panic about it – his character note.*
Guildenstern *spins.* **Rosencrantz** *studies coin.*

Rosencrantz   Heads. *(He puts it in his bag. The process is repeated)* Heads. *(Again)* Heads. *(Again)* Heads. *(Again)* Heads.
Guildenstern *(Flipping a coin)*   There is an art to the building up of suspense.
Rosencrantz   Heads.
Guildenstern *(Flipping another)* Though it can be done by luck alone.
Rosencrantz   Heads.
Guildenstern   If that's the word I'm after.
Rosencrantz *(Raises his head at* **Guildenstern***)* Seventy-six – love. *(Guildenstern gets up but has nowhere to go. He spins another coin over his shoulder without looking at it, his attention being directed at his environment or lack of it)* Heads.
Guildenstern   A weaker man might be moved to re-examine his faith, if in nothing else at least in the law of probability. *(He flips a coin over his shoulder as he goes to look upstage)*
Rosencrantz   Heads. *(He puts it in his bag.* **Guildenstern** *sits despondently. He takes a coin, spins it, lets it fall between his feet. He looks at it, picks it up, throws it to* **Rosencrantz** *who puts it in his bag.* **Guildenstern** *takes a third coin, spins it, catches it in his right hand, turns it over onto his left wrist, lobs it in the air, catches it with his left hand, raises his left leg, throws the coin up under it, catches it and turns it over on the top of his head, where it sits.* **Rosencrantz** *comes, looks at it, puts it in his bag)* I'm afraid –
Guildenstern   So am I.
Rosencrantz   I'm afraid it isn't your day.

3.6 Speech: prose and poetry

Don't be over-awed when first acting in Shakespeare. His lines can be just as effective today as they were when first spoken.

This scene comes from *The Merry Wives of Windsor*. Two married women have each received love letters. Having at first been excited, they have now discovered that the letters are identical. They both come from fat, old Sir John Falstaff.

With a partner, work on this scene. Try to make it realistic as well as funny.

(Enter **Mistress Ford** *and* **Mistress Page** *from opposite directions)*

Mistress Ford   Mistress Page! Trust me, I was going to your house.

Mistress Page   And, trust me, I was coming to you.

Mistress Ford   O Mistress Page, give me some counsel.

Mistress Page   What's the matter, woman?

Mistress Ford   Here, read, read. I shall think the worse of fat men as long as I have an eye to make difference of men's liking. How shall I be revenged on him? I think the best way were to entertain him with hope till the wicked fire of lust have melted him in his own grease. Did you ever hear the like?

Mistress Page   *(Comparing the two letters)*   Letter for letter, but that the name of Page and Ford differs. Here's the twin-brother of thy letter. I warrant he hath a thousand of these letters, writ with blank space for different names – sure, more – and these are of the second editions. *(She gives her letter to* **Mistress Ford***)*

Mistress Ford   Why, this is the very same: the very hand, the very words. What doth he think of us?

Mistress Page   Nay, I know not. He will never have board me in this way.

Mistress Ford   'Boarding' call you it? I'll be sure to keep him above deck.

Mistress Page   So will I. If he comes under my hatches I'll never to sea again. Let's be revenged on him.

58

Now work on this cynical speech from *As You Like It*.

> All the world's a stage,
> And all the men and women merely players:
> They have their exits and entrances;
> And one man in his time plays many parts,
> His acts being seven ages. At first the infant,
> Mewling and puking in the nurse's arms.
> And then the whining school-boy, with his satchel
> And shining morning face, creeping like snail
> Unwillingly to school. And then the lover,
> Sighing like furnace, with a woeful ballad
> Made to his mistress' eyebrow. Then a soldier,
> Full of strange oaths, and bearded like the pard,
> Jealous in honour, sudden and quick in quarrel,
> Seeking the bubble reputation
> Even in the cannon's mouth. And then the justice,
> In fair round belly with good capon lin'd,
> With eyes severe, and beard of formal cut,
> Full of wise saws and modern instances;
> And so he plays his part. The sixth age shifts
> Into the lean and slipper'd pantaloon,
> With spectacles on nose and pouch on side,
> His youthful hose well sav'd, a world too wide
> For his shrunk shank; and his manly voice,
> Turning again toward childish treble, pipes
> And whistles in his sound. Last scene of all,
> That ends this strange eventful history,
> Is second childishness and mere oblivion,
> Sans teeth, sans eyes, sans taste, sans everything.

3.7 Acting: the Elizabethan actor's life

In Elizabethan times, actors were outlaws – classed with rogues and vagabonds. In London, many gained respectability by becoming members of a company like the Lord Chamberlain's Men. Thus they were technically servants of a nobleman. This was the case with Shakespeare's actors. Many others led a precarious existence as travelling players, touring round the country, seeking an audience where they could find one.

In a modern play about the events that happen off stage in *Hamlet – Rosencrantz and Guildenstern Are Dead* by Tom Stoppard – such a group of touring players meet two Elizabethan courtiers, Rosencrantz and Guildenstern.

*(The Tragedians enter. The Spokesman ('the **Player**')*
*is the first to notice **Rosencrantz** and **Guildenstern**.)*

Player   Halt! *(The Group turns and halts. Joyously)* An
    audience. *(**Rosencrantz** and **Guildenstern** half*
    rise) Don't move! *(They sink back)* Perfect! A
    lucky thing we came along.

Rosencrantz   Why's that?

Player   Why, we grow rusty! By this time
    tomorrow we might have forgotten everything
    we ever knew. That's a thought, isn't it? *(He*
    laughs generously) We'd be back where we started
    – improvising.

Rosencrantz   Tumblers, are you?

Player   We can give you a tumble if that's your
    taste, and times being what they are. Otherwise,
    for a jingle of coin we can do you a selection of
    gory romances, full of fine cadence and corpses,
    pirated from the Italian; and it doesn't take much
    to make a jingle – even a single coin has music in
    it. *(They all flourish and bow, raggedly)*

Rosencrantz   What is your line?

Player   Tragedy, sir. Deaths and disclosures,
    universal and particular denouements both
    unexpected and inexorable, transvestite
    melodrama on all levels including the suggestive.
    We transport you into a world of intrigue and
    illusion – clowns, if you like, murderers – we can
    do you ghosts and battles, on the skirmish level,
    heroes, villains, tormented lovers – set pieces in
    the poetic vein; we can do you rapiers or rape or
    both, by all means, faithless wives and ravished
    virgins at a price, but that comes under realism
    for which there are special terms. Getting warm,
    am I?

Rosencrantz *(Doubtful)* Well, I don't know . . .

Player   It costs little to watch, and little more if you
    happen to get caught up in the action, if that's
    your taste and times being what they are . . .

Rehearse and stage this scene. Try improvising
other scenes about the life of a group of strolling
players.

    The players in the above scene are the ones
that arrive at Elsinore in Shakespeare's play,
Hamlet (see 3.4). Hamlet gives more good advice
about acting to the players.

Hamlet *(to the first **Player**)* Speak the speech I pray
    you as I pronounced it to you, trippingly on the
    tongue, but if you mouth it as many of your
    players do, I had as lief the town-crier spoke my
    lines. Nor do not saw the air too much with your
    hand thus, but use all gently, for in the very
    torrent, tempest, and as I may say whirlwind of
    your passion, you must acquire and beget a

temperance that may give it smoothness. O, it
offends me to the soul, to hear a robustious
periwig-pated fellow tear a passion to tatters, to
very rags, to split the ears of the groundlings,
who for the most part are capable of nothing but
inexplicable dumb-shows and noise!

I Player   I warrant your honour.

Hamlet   Be not too tame either, but let your own
    discretion be your tutor, suit the action to the
    word, the word to the action, with this special
    observance, that you o'erstep not the modesty of
    nature: for any thing so o'erdone is from the
    purpose of playing, whose end both at the first,
    and now, was and is, to hold as 'twere the mirror
    up to nature . . .

Work out what Hamlet means – and then
rehearse the scene.

3.8 Dance 2

Revenge plays were very popular in Elizabethan
times. They were a kind of horror play which
told of terrible deeds and the consequent revenge
sought by the friends and relatives of those who
had been killed or who had suffered in other
ways. Shakespeare's *Romeo and Juliet* and *Hamlet*
are both about revenge. A modern musical, *West
Side Story*, takes the plot of *Romeo and Juliet* but
sets it in New York and tells of rivalry and
revenge between two gangs.

    Devise a dance drama based on *West Side Story*
or one on this report which appeared in the
Guardian in 1966:

> There was a girl in a southern Italian village who
> dishonoured her husband and family by comitting
> adultery. Her father and brothers appointed
> themselves her executioners, asserting their prior
> right over her husband. She ran up the village
> street, looking for help, but every door was barred
> in her face. At the top of the street they caught her
> and killed her . . .

3.9 Directing: rehearsal

There are as many ways of conducting a
rehearsal as there are directors. Some see
themselves as chairmen who hardly say a word,
allowing all the ideas to come from the actors.
Others are dictators who instruct the cast in

every detail. Obviously a mixture is best in most cases.

There are some rules. A director must help his cast to understand the background of the play and its plot. Ideally the interpretation of a particular role comes from the actor: it is the director's job to guide that interpretation through improvisation and/or discussion. He must also help his actors to understand the relationships between characters. It is unwise for him to demonstrate. This is either because he may not do it very well or because he may do it so well that the actor has no contribution to make or may even feel inadequate. The director must always be tactful and must steadily build up the confidence of the cast. But he must also maintain discipline and avoid time-wasting, and also resolve any conflicts of interpretation. In the final resort, he is the boss!

Some directors come to rehearsal with all the moves 'blocked'. That is, with all the details of who moves where and when worked out and entered in his copy – perhaps even down to each gesture. Others allow all movement to be developed and worked out during rehearsal. It is probably best if the director does work out basic moves in advance – where characters enter and exit and where any other major business, for example 'deaths', fights and key dialogues will take place – but allows incidental movements to build up gradually during rehearsals.

3.10   Documentary: Shakespeare's life

Plan, research, rehearse and present a documentary on the life and work of William Shakespeare. Think carefully of all the elements you could include – excerpts from his plays, music, dance, improvised scenes, songs, demonstrations of how his plays were staged and some information and illustration of the history of the period. The following account of a visit to London made in 1598 may give you further ideas:

> Without the city are some theatres, where English actors represent almost every day comedies and tragedies to very numerous audiences; these are concluded with variety of dances, accompanied by excellent music and the excessive applause of those that are present. Not far from one of these theatres, which are all built of wood, lies the royal barge, close to the river Thames. It has two splendid cabins, beautifully ornamented with glass windows, painting and gilding; it is kept upon dry ground, and sheltered from the weather.
> There is still another place, built in the form of a theatre, which serves for the baiting of bears and bulls. They are fastened behind, and then worried by those great English dogs and mastiffs, but not without great risk to the dogs from the teeth of the one and the horns of the other; and it sometimes happens they are killed upon the spot.
> Fresh ones are immediately supplied in the places of those that are wounded or tired. To this entertainment there often follows that of whipping a blinded bear, which is performed by five or six men, standing in a circle with whips, which they exercise upon him without any mercy. Although he cannot escape from them because of his chain, he nevertheless defends himself, vigorously throwing down all who come within his reach and are not active enough to get out of it, and tearing the whips out of their hands and breaking them. At these spectacles and everywhere else, the English are constantly smoking the Nicotian weed which in America is called Tobaca – others call it Patum – and generally in this manner; they have pipes on purpose made of clay, into the farther end of which they put the herb, so dry that it may be rubbed into powder, and lighting it, they draw the smoke into their mouths, which they puff out again through their nostrils, like funnels, along with it plenty of phlegm and defluxion from the head. In these theatres, fruits, such as apples, pears and nuts, according to the season, are carried about to be sold, as well as wine and ale.

> Paul Hentzner

3.11 Design: sketches

As soon as he begins his research, the good designer will start making lots of rough sketches of architectural styles, types of furniture and costume outlines, to use when discussing the style of the production with the director.

Remember: on many stages it is the outline of a costume or piece of stage furniture rather than its detail that will create the strongest effect.

In the past, it was the fashion to fill the stage with every realistic detail of a setting. Now, as in Shakespeare's time, it is often a matter of knowing how to select the one detail that will convey a location to an audience.

As practice, draw rough sketches of one piece of stage furniture or scenery that would suggest each of the following:

the interior of a royal palace;
an Elizabethan street at night;
the garden of an English country house;
Athens;
a very bleak stretch of heathland;
Rome;
the interior of an alehouse.

Consult reference books where necessary.

Costume: accessories

[th]ough it is not necessary for stage costumes to [refle]ct every detail of the original, some well-chosen accessories can be very helpful in suggesting period. The following will be useful in making accessories to accompany Elizabethan, and other period, costumes:

stiff cartridge paper, cardboard, old buttons, beads, cord and string, tissue paper, felt, unwanted leather, pigskin-type materials, a stapler, scissors, adhesive, and a tape-measure.

When making a particular item, first try to find illustrations of it. Then make rough sketches. If necessary, measure the person who is to wear the item. For example, measure a person's head *before* attempting to make a crown that will fit!

The above materials can be used to make: crowns of various periods; purses; decorated belts; armlets; necklaces; bracelets; fans; brooches; armour – especially breastplates, greaves and armlets.

Silver and gold paint, applied either with a brush or from an aerosol, can give cardboard a metallic look – though grey paint may be as effective in some lighting.

Old wellingtons and plimsolls are worth collecting so that they can on occasion be turned into period footwear. Experiment by turning down the tops of wellingtons to make riding boots, or by building up plimsolls with felt to make medieval short boots. Buckles can add period to modern slip-on shoes.

Practise using and moving with such accessories. How would they have been used? How do they alter movement? Rehearse carefully any movements in armour.

3.13 Lighting: control

It is the control which brings all the varied stage lighting circuits together and makes them an instrument of artistic expression. No matter how well directed or appropriately focused the Fresnel, the Profile spot, or the Floods, the stage picture will be made by operating the dimmers from the control desk.

Dimmers are used to facilitate the change, gradual or fast, from one picture to another. They also allow a lantern or group of lanterns to be left only partly on to create a particular effect.

1 Assembling

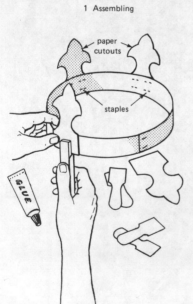

2 Strengthening

Tape wire to the outside of each upright and edge with cord.

3 Decorating

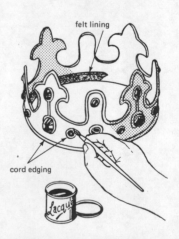

Use beads covered with coloured foil or sweet wrappers for the jewels. Paint the rest with metallic lacquer.

Many halls and theatres still have manual 'slider' dimmers. The disadvantage of these is that you need several arms to operate them, as you will probably have to move several of the sliders on any one cue. To ensure precision and smoothness in these changes it is really necessary to have presetting facilities to allow the precise intensity levels required for the next stage picture to be preset in advance of the lighting change. Conventional Preset Controls have one set of dimmers levers to hold the lighting balance for the picture now on the stage, and another set, at least, on which to preset the picture which is to follow.

Mini–2 is a direct development of the Rank Strand thyristor dimmers and preset controls used by the large theatres, but designed to suit the smaller stage. Thyristor dimming means finger-tip-operated control panels which can be sited conveniently in the wings or anywhere in the theatre.

The facility to preset the lighting scene has been the greatest single advance in fifty years of stage lighting. A duplicated set of control levers on the Mini–2 enables the next scene to be set up whilst holding the existing lighting picture. Master fader levers provide a smooth change-over from one stage picture to the next on cue.

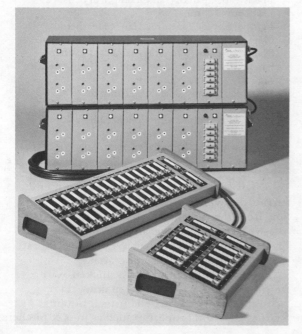

3.14 Music

The Royal Shakespeare Company is very much aware of the part that music can play in a stage show. Guy Wolfenden is their music director. His work is described by Trevor Nunn:

> Staging a theatre production is a collective process; the director, the actors, the designer and the composer must be able to work together, to understand each other, take from each other and give to each other. For the theatre, Guy Wolfenden is the complete composer. He has the rare ability to create within a precisely defined context, and yet to retain his own individuality. His music is always a very personal response to the text, and to the director's intentions. He is part performer, part conductor, part scholar, part director. He writes music timed to the second, provides fanfares, jigs, pavanes, dirges, songs, alarums and excursions. He is aware that most actors are bad dancers; that a scene change in rehearsal might suddenly have to be ten seconds longer or twenty seconds shorter, that some plays demand brass and percussion and others a consort of viols, or a saxophone or a crumhorn, that this one is better recorded and that that one must be live.

Try to build up a collection of music that will help you when working on improvised or scripted drama. Look for records that will suggest the period and location in which your work is set.

Look also for suitable opportunities of including live music in your presentations: encourage those members of your group who can play the guitar, piano or any other instrument, to improvise and compose incidental music. Those who think they are not musical should be brave and experiment with percussion instruments!

3.15 Make–up: character

Ageing a young face so that it looks convincingly old in close-up is not easy. Even harder in some ways is suggesting middle age. However, some things can be done quite easily to add or change character.

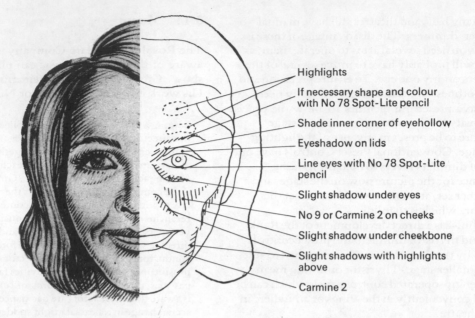

Highlights

If necessary shape and colour with No 78 Spot-Lite pencil

Shade inner corner of eyehollow

Eyeshadow on lids

Line eyes with No 78 Spot-Lite pencil

Slight shadow under eyes

No 9 or Carmine 2 on cheeks

Slight shadow under cheekbone

Slight shadows with highlights above

Carmine 2

To broaden a face:
style the hair so that the outline is as wide as possible; mask the eyebrows with No 5 (see 2.15) and paint in false ones at a lower level; take the outline of the lips outwards.

To lengthen a face:
brush the hair well back from the brow; add highlights on the brow; raise the eyebrows; highlight the cheekbones and shade in the cheeks.

To give the impression of a middle-aged woman, try using 52 or 53 as foundation; some 2½ to give a pinkish appearance, if required; 5 or 2 for highlights; 9 for cheeks; Carmine 2 or 3 for the lips. Powder with rose or neutral blending powder.

Always link practice make-up sessions with movement and speech work. Make-up cannot create an illusion on its own. It is still up to the actor to convey an image by his movements, mannerisms and speech. The make-up is not more than an aid.

3.16 Stagecraft: furniture

Although there was almost no scenery in the Elizabethan theatre, there was some stage furniture. Chairs and stools brought on stage indicated we were now indoors, a throne indicated a palace and so on. Some of this furniture may have been fairly elaborate. These are some of the items in a 'list of properties' belonging to one company of actors in 1598:

1 rock, 1 cage, 1 tomb, 1 Hell mouth, 2 moss banks, 1 beacon, 1 bay tree, 1 tree of golden apples.
1 bedstead, 1 pair of stairs, 1 chime of bells, 1 sackbut, 2 coffins.
1 globe, 1 golden sceptre, 2 fans of feathers. Neptune's fork and garland, Mercury's wings.
8 lances, 3 clubs, 1 wooden hatchet, 1 leather hatchet, 17 foils, 1 greeve armour, 1 helmet with a dragon, 1 shield, 1 gilt spear.
1 wooden canopy, 1 snake, 3 timbrels.
1 bull's head, 1 dragon in Faustus, 1 lion, 2 lion's heads, 1 great horse with his legs, 1 lion skin, 1 bear skin.
1 Pope's mitre, 3 Imperial crowns, 1 plain crown, 1 ghost's crown.

When making stage furniture, always remember to find out what it will look like under the lights, and from the audience. Remember too that it is often easier to 'decorate' an ordinary chair with paier mâché moulding than to build an elaborate period chair or throne from scratch.

Layers of papier mâché on a chicken-wire framework is a useful way of making stage sculpture, e.g. ornamental busts, fountains, statues etc., and properties such as jugs & pitchers.

66

It is well worth building up a basic collection of furniture, or a catalogue of where items may be borrowed from, for use in productions and presentations. Which of the items on the list above would be useful? What other items do you need regularly?

3.17   Criticism

The job of the theatre critic is to describe what he sees and hears. It is his job to decide what a play is about – its storyline, themes and 'message'; and then to assess whether the company has staged it effectively and pleasingly.

The *Sunday Times* critic Raymond Mortimer described the task of a book critic in this way:

> Reviewers have to capture and to retain the readers' attention. Good judgement and bright ideas are not enough. You must also give an edge to your words, making them pleasing to the ear, lucid, neat and succinct. Few of us can achieve an easy-seeming style free from clichés, without hard work and patient revision.
>
> Tone also is important. Some editors like reviews to be either black or white. I don't. That is a cheap path to popularity. Begin by absorbing the point of view taken by the author you have to discuss! Instead of acting as counsel for the defence or the prosecution, try to produce a judicial summing–up, including the good points in a feeble book and the feeble points in a good one!

How can that advice be adapted to apply to serve as advice to a theatre critic?

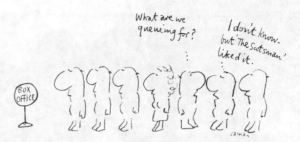

Write reviews of productions you see. After you have written them, compare them with newspaper reviews of the same productions. NB Raymond Mortimer added the point:

> The savage review is a too easy form of fun, usually better left, I believe, to the young.

Learn from reviews of your own work!

3.18   Project: Doctor Faustus

Dr Faustus is the most famous play written by one of Shakespeare's contemporaries, Christopher Marlowe, and tells the legend of the man who sold his soul to the devil in return for twenty–four years of power. It makes a good subject for a stage presentation involving improvisation, dance, mime and varied use of lighting and other effects.

The story is as follows:

Doctor Faustus has become bored with studying science. He wants even more power and knowledge. He thus decides to call up Mephostophilis, an evil spirit and servant of the devil. Faustus's 'Good Angel' tries to persuade him to have nothing to do with the devil, and certainly not to enter into any bargain with him.

The 'Bad Angel' points out all the attractions of power and wealth and knowledge that can be gained by serving the devil.

Faustus does summon up Mephostophilis and signs a bargain – in blood. The devil can have Faustus's soul after twenty-four years – in return for which Mephostophilis will attend Faustus for that period of twenty-four years and provide him with all he wishes.

Faustus is given various books containing all knowledge, all spells and incantations; he is introduced to the seven deadly sins; and is taken on a tour of the world. Finally, Mephostophilis presents him with the most beautiful woman who ever lived – Helen of Troy. But by now the twenty-four years have passed and the play ends with the devil coming to seize the terrified Faustus, in order to drag him down to hell.

This is the scene from Marlowe's play in which Faustus signs away his soul:

Faustus When Mephostophilis shall stand by me
  What god can hurt me?
  Mephostophilis, come
  And bring glad tiding from great Lucifer.
  Is't not midnight? Come Mephostophilis,
  Veni, veni Mephostophilis.
  (Enter **Mephostophilis***)*
  Now tell me what saith Lucifer thy lord?
Mephostophilis That I shall wait on Faustus whilst he lives,
  So he will buy my services with his soul.
Faustus Already Faustus hath hazarded that for thee.
Mephostophilis But now thou must bequeath it solemnly,
  And write a deed of gift with thine own blood.
Faustus Ay Mephostophilis, I'll give it him.
Mephostophilis Then Faustus, stab thine arm courageously
  And bind thy soul, that at some certain day
  Great Lucifer may claim it as his own,
  And then be thou as great as Lucifer.
Faustus Lo Mephostophilis, for love of thee
  (stabs his arm)
  Faustus hath cut his arm, and with his proper blood
  Assures his soul to be great Lucifer's

Chief lord and regent of perpetual night
  View here this blood that trickles from mine arm,
  And let it be propitious for my wish.
Mephostophilis But Faustus
  Write it in manner of a deed of gift.
Faustus Ay, so I will. *(Writes)*
  But Mephostophilis,
  My blood congeals, and I can write no more.
Mephostophilis I'll fetch thee fire to dissolve it straight.
Faustus What might the staying of my blood portend?
  Is it unwilling I should write this bill?
  Why streams it not, that I may write afresh?
  'Faustus gives to thee his soul': ah, there it stayed!
  Why should'st thou not? Is not thy soul thine own?
  Then write again: 'Faustus gives to thee his soul'.
  (Enter **Mephostophilis** *with the chafer of fire)*
Mephostophilis See Faustus here is fire, set it on.
Faustus So, now the blood begins to clear again:
  (writes again)
  Now will I make an end immediately.
Mephostophilis What will not I do to obtain his soul!
Faustus Consummatum est: this bill is ended,
  And Faustus hath bequeathed his soul to Lucifer.
Mephostophilis *(aside)* I'll fetch him somewhat to delight his mind.
  (Enter **Devils**, *giving crowns and rich apparel to* **Faustus**: *they dance, and then depart.)*

You may wish to include that scene in your version of the story, or re-work it in your own words. Discuss fully how you can stage the other parts of the story. You will probably wish to include these characters:

  Faustus; Mephostophilis; Faustus's Good Angel; Faustus's Bad Angel; the Seven Deadly Sins – Pride, Covetousness, Envy, Wrath, Gluttony, Sloth and Lechery; Helen of Troy; other devils.

Other characters in Marlowe's play that you might wish to include are:

  Wagner, Faustus's servant; Lucifer, the prince of devils; various characters whom Faustus meets on his travels.

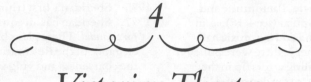

4
Victorian Theatre

4.1 Stages: proscenium

The proscenium stage consists basically of a
platform behind a permanent opening. (See unit
1.2 for the derivation of the word 'proscenium'.)
Usually a curtain can be lowered, or a pair of
curtains closed, and so separate the stage from
the auditorium. Even when the curtains are
open, there is a sense that the stage and
auditorium are separate 'rooms' – the audience is
looking through a picture frame into another
world. This separation is increased in many
theatres by the presence of a 'pit' which can
contain musicians – the orchestra pit.

The disadvantage of this separation of actors
and audience is that the actors must work hard to
'project' their performance from the stage to the
auditorium, and their acting can seem forced or
artificial. Its advantage is that very realistic box–
sets can be constructed on the stage and elaborate
effects devised.

The proscenium arch theatre was very
popular for many years but there is no reason
why we should think that this type of theatre is a
'proper' theatre any more than any other.

4.2 Theatres: Victorian

From the Restoration onwards (see unit 4.3)
theatres became smaller, roofed buildings. A
typical theatre of this period may have seated
only 500, and the distance from the stage to the
back of the theatre was perhaps no more than
thirty–six feet. The next development was the
proscenium arch.

By Victorian times theatres had begun to
grow in size again, and there was a complete
separation of stage and auditorium. In 1812,
when Drury Lane was rebuilt after a fire, it had a
capacity of 3200 and a proscenium opening of
thirty-three feet. The size of such theatres made

it difficult for speech to be heard or for detailed acting to be appreciated. Consequently the theatres favoured spectacle. Pantomime and harlequinade became popular (see 4.18), as in later years did melodrama and the music hall.

Besides elaborate scenery, there were pulleys in plenty, capable of hauling actors up in the 'sky', there were elaborate trap doors and 'lifts', and there were various smoke effects.

Alongside the move towards the spectacular, there was increasing realism. Settings had to be historically accurate, especially as new realistic plays became popular.

4.3 Dramatists: from the Restoration to Early Realist

This table indicates some of the key writers and other theatrical events of this period.

1642 The Puritans, who believed theatres were immoral, succeed in closing the theatres in England.

1660 The Restoration of the Monarchy: the theatres re-open.

1660s In France, Molière's greatest comedies and Racine's greatest tragedies are first performed.

1690s The Restoration playwrights sweep to popularity with their comedies of manners and intrigue – especially Sir George Etherege, William Wycherley, William Congreve and George Farquhar.

1747 David Garrick, one of the most famous actor-managers, takes over the running of Drury Lane Theatre in London.

1773 Goldsmith's comedy *She Stoops to Conquer* is first performed.

1775 Sheridan's first triumph, *The Rivals*.

1777 Sheridan has an equal success with *School for Scandal*. These plays have all the wit and elegance of the Restoration comedies but lack the coarseness and vulgarity.

R. B. Sheridan

1820s Melodrama becomes popular.

1836 In Russia, Nikolai Gogol writes *The Government Inspector*, a hilarious satire on petty officials.

1850 The first performance of a play by Henrik Ibsen. This Norwegian writer is often called the father of modern theatre. His plays may lack humour but they are superbly constructed, very moving and richly symbolic. His most famous and powerful ones – *A Doll's House, Ghosts, The Wild Duck, Hedda Gabler*; were first performed in the 1870s and 1880s.

1860s Music hall becomes popular in England.

1880s Chekhov becomes successful in Russia and elsewhere with his tragi-comedies.

David Garrick

1895   Oscar Wilde's *The Importance of Being
Earnest* is a hit in London.

Oscar Wilde

1895 onwards: George Bernard Shaw achieves
popularity with plays that debate topical and
other issues, for example *Mrs Warren's
Profession* deals with prostitution; *The Doctor's
Dilemma* with medical abuses, *Major Barbara*
with the Salvation Army and wealth and
poverty; *Pygmalion* with class differences.
Shaw wrote many other plays, and all make
serious points but are also very witty.

George Bernard Shaw

73

4.4 Improvisation: towards performance

At some point, you will be ready to start developing and revising improvisations in order to present them to an audience. This point will come when you can repeat an improvisation without its nature altering. This does not mean that it must be exactly the same every time you repeat it – far from it. What it means is that it should always have the same qualities of involvement and belief that it did the first time you acted it out.

Don't try presenting improvisations to an audience if you tend to react to their laughter or applause, if you tend to slip out of character, or if you start playing a serious improvisation for laughs. Prepare for this sort of presentation by working in different groupings. First show your work to other groups in your class or set, then gradually get used to working in larger groups; don't try to leap from working in fours to working as a group of sixteen. Always decide in advance who will end a 'public' improvisation.

Begin by presenting improvisations in the round, move to working on a thrust stage – and then progress to a proscenium stage. Look at the diagrams. NB Directional lighting, props and costumes will help.

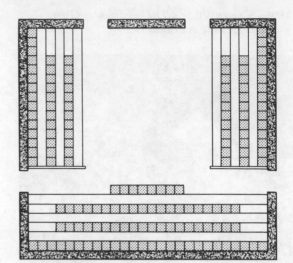

'Thrust' or Elizabethan stage

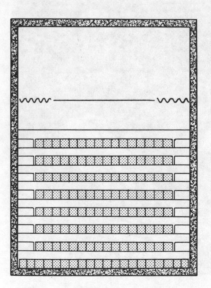

Proscenium or 'end' stage

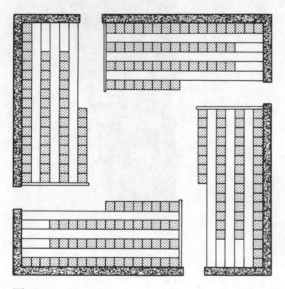

Theatre-in-the-round

Why is it easier to begin by presenting improvisations in the round? What are the problems of improvising on a proscenium stage? Who are you working to? Each other or the audience?

Now try developing an improvisation that went well. But first, try this warm-up game:

74

Tag-improvisation. Two teams, of at least two players each, sit facing each other on either side of the 'ring'. The referee announces the location of the scene, for example a restaurant, railway station, supermarket checkout, fun fair, police station; and gives an 'identity' to the first two contestants, for example clumsy waiter, pompous businessman, forgiving clergyman, suspicious detective.

The improvisation is then started, possibly by the referee giving an opening line, and continues until one of the contestants 'tags' — as in tag wrestling — another member of his team who must then replace him or her and carry on the scene. The departing improviser should introduce the newcomer: 'Ah, here is the criminal you're looking for!' or 'This is my friend, Mrs Brown, she knows all about hydrangeas!'.

4.5 Movement:

JABBERWOCKY

'Twas brillig, and the slithy toves
    Did gyre and gimble in the wabe;
All mimsy were the borogoves,
    And the mome raths outgrabe.

'Beware the Jabberwock, my son!
    The jaws that bite, the claws that catch'
Beware the Jubjub bird, and shun
    The frumious Bandersnatch!'

He took his vorpal sword in hand:
    Long time the manxome foe he sought —
So rested he by the Tumtum tree,
    And stood awhile in thought.

And as in uffish thought he stood,
    The Jabberwock, with eyes of flame,
Came whiffling through the tulgey wood,
    And burbled as it came.

One, two! One, two! And through and through
    The vorpal blade went snicker snack!
He left it dead, and with its head
    He went galumphing back.

'And hast thou slain the Jabberwock'
    Come to my arms, my beamish boy!
O frabjous day! Callooh! Callay!
    He chortled in his joy.

Jabberwocky from *Through the Looking Glass* by

Lewis Carroll is not just a nonsense poem. Humpty Dumpty explains part of it to Alice:

    '"Brillig" means four o'clock in the afternoon — the time when you begin broiling things for dinner.'
    'That'll do very well,' said Alice: 'and "slithy"?'
    'Well, "slithy" means "lithe and slimy". "Lithe" is the same as "active". You see it's like a portmanteau — there are two meanings packed up into one word.'
    'I see it now,' Alice remarked thoughtfully: 'and what are "toves"?'
    'Well, "toves" are something like badgers — they're something like lizards — and they're something like corkscrews.'
    'They must be very curious-looking creatures.'
    'They are that,' said Humpty Dumpty: 'also they make their nests under sun-dials — also they live on cheese.'
    'And what's to "gyre" and to "gimble"?'
    'To "gyre" is to go round and round like a gyro-scope. To "gimble" is to make holes like a gimblet.'

Using percussion or suitable radiophonic or traditional music as an accompaniment, act out the story of the poem as a solo movement exercise. Remember to work at different levels and with a variety of tempo.

Next work on the poem as a group exercise, with the following roles:

narrator, toves, borogoves, mome raths, the Jabberwock – which might be played by two people, the Jubjub bird, the Bandersnatch, and the hero who triumphs over the Jabberwock.

4.6 Speech: monologues

The famous Russian playwright Anton Chekhov (1860–1904) is chiefly famous for the clever mixture of tragedy and comedy in his plays. In many respects the *situation* of his characters is tragic, but they themselves are also often absurdly comic.

Beside full-length plays such as *The Seagull* and *The Cherry Orchard*, he wrote a number of short sketches including *Smoking is Bad for You*. This monologue, that is a play with only one character on stage, makes fun of a type of entertainment common in the nineteenth century: the 'improving' or moral lecture. NB The lecturer is absurdly incompetent but as a poor hen-pecked husband should win our pity.

When working on this much-shortened version of the sketch, make sure you can imagine what is going on in the character's mind; practise how he will talk and walk; decide what mannerisms or habits he has; and remember that he must be heard at the back of the hall – but that he will speak in a variety of ways as he wanders from the subject and then returns to it.

(**Ivan Nyukhin** *has long side-whiskers, wears an old, worn coat. His wife keeps a girls' boarding school*)

Nyukhin Ladies, and er, in a manner of speaking, gentlemen. *(Strokes his side-whiskers)* It's been suggested to the wife that I should lecture here in aid of charity on some topic of general interest. I don't see why not. If I'm to lecture, I'll lecture – I just couldn't care less. *(Sips a glass of water)* As the subject of my lecture today, I've chosen, as it were, the harmful effects of smoking on the human race. I'm a smoker myself, actually. But the wife told me to give today's lecture on why tobacco's bad for you, so what's the use of arguing? About tobacco as such, I just couldn't care less. But I suggest, ladies and gentlemen, that you attend to my present lecture with all due seriousness, or something worse may happen. I should like to ask the doctors in my audience to pay particular attention. My lecture is a mine of useful information for them, since nicotine not only has harmful effects, but is also used in medicine. For instance, if you put a fly in a snuff-box it will die – from a nervous breakdown, probably. Tobacco is, essentially, a plant. When I lecture my right eye usually twitches, but you can ignore that – it's pure nervousness.
I'm a nervous wreck by and large, and this eye-twitching business started back in September 1889, on the thirteenth of the month – the very day when my wife gave birth, in a manner of speaking, to our fourth daughter, Barbara. My daughters were all born on the 13th.

Actually *(with a look at his watch)*, time being short, let's not wander from the subject in hand. My wife runs a school of music, I might add, and a private boarding-school – well, not a boarding-school exactly, but something in that line. Between you and me, my wife likes to complain of being hard up, but she's got a tidy bit salted away – a cool forty or fifty thousand – while I haven't a penny to my name, not a bean. But what's the use of talking? I'm the school matron. I buy food, keep an eye on the servants, do the accounts, make-up exercise books, exterminate bed-bugs, take the wife's dog for walks and catch mice. However *(looks at his watch)*, we've somewhat erred and strayed from our subject. By the way, I forgot to say that besides being matron in the wife's school of music, I also have the job of teaching mathematics, physics, chemistry, geography, history, singing scales, literature and all that. The wife charges extra for dancing, singing and drawing, though I'm also the singing and dancing master.

Our school of music is at Number Thirteen, Five Dogs Lane. That's probably why I've always had such bad luck – living at Number Thirteen. My daughters were born on the thirteenth of the month too, and the house has thirteen windows. But what's the use of talking? I'm a complete failure, I've grown old and stupid. *(Makes a suitable gesture to indicate drinking)* Yes, drinking. One glass is enough to make me drunk, I might add. It feels good, but indescribably sad at the same time. Somehow the days of my youth come back to me, I somehow long – more than you can possibly imagine – to escape. *(Carried away)* To run away, leave everything behind and run away without a backward glance. Where to? Who cares? If only I could escape from this rotten, vulgar, tawdry existence that's turned me into a pathetic old clown and imbecile! Escape from this stupid, petty, vicious, nasty, spiteful, mean old cow of a wife who's made my life a misery for thirty-three years! Escape from the music, the kitchen, my wife's money and all these vulgar trivialities! Oh, to stop somewhere in the depths of the country and just stand there like a tree or a post or a scarecrow on some vegetable plot under the broad sky, and watch the quiet, bright moon above you all night long and forget, forget! How I'd love to lose my memory!

How I'd love to tear off this rotten old coat that I got married in thirty years ago *(tears off his coat)* the one I always wear when I lecture for charity. So much for you! *(Stamps on the coat)* Once I was young and clever and went to college. I had dreams and I felt like a human being. Now I want nothing – nothing but a bit of peace and quiet. *(Glancing to one side, quickly puts on his tail-coat)* I say, my wife's out there in the wings. She's turned up and she's waiting for me there. *(Looks at his watch)* Time's up. If she asks, please, please tell her the lecture was, er – that the imbecile, meaning me, behaved with dignity. *(Looks to one side and coughs)* She's looking this way. *(Raising his voice)* On the supposition that tobacco contains the terrible poison to which I have just alluded, smoking should on no account be indulged in. I shall therefore venture to hope, in a manner of speaking, that some benefit may accrue from this lecture on 'Smoking is Bad for you'. *(Aside:)* That's the end. *(Bows and struts out majestically)*

4.7 Acting: pace

It is important that in any production the pace is varied. A scene quickly becomes monotonous if every pause is exactly the same length – or if there are no pauses at all. A pause can often heighten an effect – but obviously it is possible to over-do such silences.

Work on this scene from *The Importance of Being Earnest* by Oscar Wilde. It is set in the garden of a country house. Cecily is entertaining Gwendolen to tea. Both are wealthy, upper-class young ladies. Each believes the other has captured the affections of the young man with whom she is in love – and consequently they detest each other, but nevertheless they try to preserve their manners.

Read and rehearse it; then work on the characterisation. Play it with fairly long pauses. Which of the pauses add to the comedy? Where are they unhelpful? Where must you add pace? What does the butler add to the scene? NB Take care he doesn't upstage Cecily and Gwendolen.

When rehearsing a scene, director and actors need to be able to refer easily to different areas of the stage. The diagram overleaf shows the commonly used terms.

*(Enter the butler, **Merriman**. He carries a salver, table cloth and plate stand.)*
Merriman Shall I lay tea here as usual, Miss?
Cecily *(Sternly, in a calm voice)* Yes, as usual.
*(**Merriman** begins to clear table and lay cloth. A long pause. **Cecily** and **Gwendolen** glare at each other.)*

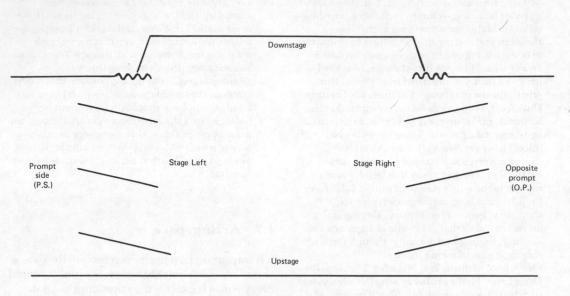

Which areas will be called 'Downstage Right',
'Up Left' and 'Down Centre'?

Gwendolen Are there many interesting walks in the vicinity, Miss Cardew?

Cecily Oh! yes! a great many. From the top of one of the hills quite close one can see five counties.

Gwendolen Five counties! I don't think I should like that; I hate crowds.

Cecily *(Sweetly)* I suppose that is why you live in town?

(Gwendolen *bites her lip, and beats her foot nervously with her parasol.)*

Gwendolen *(Looking round)* Quite a well–kept garden this is, Miss Cardew.

Cecily So glad you like it, Miss Fairfax.

Gwendolen I had no idea there were any flowers in the country.

Cecily Oh, flowers are as common here, Miss Fairfax, as people are in London.

Gwendolen Personally, I cannot understand how anybody manages to exist in the country, if anybody who is anybody does. The country always bores me to death.

Cecily Ah! This is what the newspapers call agricultural depression, is it not? I believe the aristocracy are suffering very much from it just at present. It is almost an epidemic amongst them, I have been told. May I offer you some tea, Miss Fairfax?

Gwendolen *(With elaborate politeness)* Thank you. *(Aside)* Detestable girl! But I require tea!

Cecily *(Sweetly)* Sugar?

Gwendolen *(Superciliously)* No, thank you. Sugar is not fashionable any more.

(Cecily *looks angrily at her, takes up the tongs and puts four lumps of sugar into the cup)*

Cecily *(Severely)* Cake or bread and butter?

Gwendolen *(In a bored manner)* Bread and butter, please. Cake is rarely seen at the best houses nowadays.

Cecily *(Cuts a very large slice of cake and puts it on the tray)* Hand that to Miss Fairfax.

(Merriman *does so, and goes out.* **Gwendolen** *drinks the tea and makes a grimace. Puts down cup at once, reaches out her hand to the bread and butter, looks at it, and finds it is cake. Rises in indignation.)*

Gwendolen You have filled my tea with lumps of sugar, and though I asked most distinctly for bread and butter, you have given me cake. I am known for the gentleness of my disposition, and the extraordinary sweetness of my nature, but I warn you, Miss Cardew, you may go too far.

Cecily *(Rising)* To save my poor, innocent, trusting boy from the machinations of any other girl there are no lengths to which I would not go.

4.8 Mime

Mime means 'acting without words'. It also means creating imaginary 'props' in the eyes of your audience. The important thing to remember in mime is that you must pick objects up before you start using them, and you must put them down when you have finished with them. Having put them down, always show the audience your palms to stress that your hand is now 'empty'.

Practise picking up, throwing and catching, and then putting down:

> a tennis ball;
> a table tennis ball;
> a marble.

Remember: show the audience your empty hand after each exercise.

Now practise with a bottle of wine and a glass. Together with a corkscrew, they are on a table in front of you. Examine them and show them to the audience. Now pick up the bottle and the corkscrew. Draw the cork. Put the bottle down, pick up the glass, pick up the bottle again and, holding the glass level with your eye, pour a glass of wine. Remember the length of the neck of the bottle and hold the glass steady as it fills. Put down the bottle and enjoy the wine. Put down the glass. NB Never rush when miming.

Now pick up an axe – it is heavy. Feel its weight as you swing it over your shoulder. Now swing it down onto a log. The shock of the axe hitting the log will send a small reaction through your hands, arms and trunk. Wrench the axe free and repeat.

Put your hands flat against a real wall. Push against it. Note where the effort is felt in the body – the back, the legs, the neck. Now try miming the same exercise. Practise until the object gives way and you lose, and then quickly recover, your balance. Now imagine you are trapped in a cube. Explore its interior surfaces, then try to push your way out of it.

With a partner, work out mimes for these words – don't mouth the words:

> you, me, yes, no, come here, I'm angry,
> I'm sorry, you make me laugh, I'm afraid,
> forgive me.

In pairs, mime handling and dropping a precious object which belongs to one of you; going to the ice rink; two shy people getting changed on a beach to go swimming; putting up a tent on a windy day; cooking a meal; having a meal in a posh restaurant; a bored husband and enthusiastic wife at the hat counter of a department store.

Work now in character. Mime different characters getting up in the morning. Try to show their work by your mime, for example a policeman, a coal-miner and a king.

In groups, develop and mime this story: A young man is in love with a beautiful girl. They are very happy together. A press gang arrives in town. They look around the town. They find and seize the man; there is a very sad parting. He is taken to a ship. He begins to enjoy life at sea. Meanwhile, she is alone and love-sick. There is a battle at sea and the young man is killed. News is brought to the girl; she is heart-broken and left all alone.

Work out a mime for a white-faced clown. It should be funny but end tragically – so that we are genuinely moved by it.

4.9 Directing: final rehearsal

Plan the final rehearsal schedule well in advance and make sure everyone involved knows the precise times they will be required.

Your last rehearsals with the actors will include a complete run through of the play – these rehearsals will involve several of the backstage staff because by now you will be using many of the properties. Then come the last three rehearsals.

School Play: "Comedy of Errors"
Final Rehearsals

Monday
1.30 pm Room 13 Meeting for all technical staff
4.15 pm Final run-through of Acts IV & V
(with all props and sound effects; no make-up)

Tuesday
Stage crew & technicians as directed
Technical Rehearsal
3.30 pm
Remember to bring sandals, belts etc.

Wednesday
1.30 pm Room 13 Meeting for Cast
4.15 pm Costumes (as detailed by Mrs Brown)
4.30 pm on stage Costume Call + Make-up
4.45 pm Photo Call (+ local paper)
5.30 pm Dining hall Sandwiches for all involved
6.00 pm Make-up check
6.15 pm First Dress Rehearsal

Thursday
12.30 pm Room 13 Meeting for all technical staff –
Director's and S.M.'s notes
1.30 pm Room 13 Meeting for cast – Director's notes
6.15 pm Costumes / Make-up / Set Dressing
7.00 pm Second Dress Rehearsal
(First, Second & Third formers may attend)

D.S.

Technical rehearsal

All the technical staff are required at this rehearsal, and this is their deadline. All lighting, properties, scenery, effects, etc. should be complete by now.

Some directors like to take each department in turn. For example, they rehearse all the lighting changes, then the sound effects, then all the scenery and furniture changes, and so on. Others prefer to work through all the cues in order.

After the technical rehearsal, the director should check with the stage manager that all is working correctly and efficiently.

First dress rehearsal

It is usual to begin this with a costume parade to check that all is well; then a photo-call and a rehearsal of the curtain call. Then comes a complete run through of the production. The director will give any last 'notes' between acts and also at the end. If there is a real disaster, this is the last occasion when a rehearsal can be stopped.

Second dress rehearsal

This should be a complete run through, as though an audience were present. It is also a good time to praise and encourage your cast and technicians!

Then comes the first night, when the director's work is officially over – though he may need to give the occasional note to keep the performance up to scratch. His job now is mainly to check that standards are maintained and perhaps improved upon, and that enthusiasm is kept alive.

4.10   Documentary: Victorian life

Using as many sources as possible, research and compile a documentary that illustrates an aspect of Victorian life. It could be about life in a city or about working in the mines; it could be about the theatres or music halls; or it could be about school life in Victorian times.

One boarding school used letters and newspaper editorials like the following to devise a documentary play about a typhoid epidemic that happened at the school in 1876:

From the editorial in *The Times*, January 13th 1876:
Typhoid, or 'enteric', fever is the most common fever in this country. It destroyed the life of the Prince Consort in 1861 and nearly ended that of the Prince of Wales five years ago.
The fever is reproduced mainly in three ways:
– first, by poisoned sewage obtaining direct access to drinking water and so being swallowed.
– secondly, by the poisoned gas escaping from the sewers into water mains so that it is absorbed by the water, and so swallowed.
– and thirdly by the poisoned gas making its way through badly trapped drains into dwelling or sleeping rooms, and so being breathed by the occupants.
It destroys an average of about ten to twelve thousand people annually in England, and sickens and endangers about one hundred thousand more.

TO THE EDITOR OF THE LANCET

Dear Sir,

A relative of mine recently received a letter from Uppingham, telling him his son was suffering from a mild form of fever, said to be due to the excessively wet weather in the Midland counties. My relative was alarmed and asked me to go down to Uppingham at once. I found the boy with a temperature of over 105 degrees fahrenheit and clearly suffering from typhoid fever.

There is a large epidemic at Uppingham and the school term is still being allowed to continue. I complain of the Headmaster for permitting this, for shutting his eyes to the real nature of the disease and not telling the parents when the fever first broke out.

I am, sir, yours obediently, 'A Doctor'.

This is one of the scenes from the play.

(The Sanitorium. **Nash**, *a boy, is lying on a bed in agony: writhing, in delirium, crying out. A dim light.* **Matron** *is bathing his forehead.)*

Matron   Stephen, lie still. Do try to . . . oh God, have mercy on us all. There, there, Stephen, my poor boy . . .

(A master arrives with the boy's parents)

Christian   Matron, this is Mr and Mrs Nash . . .

Mrs Nash   Stephen! *(She runs to him and tries to comfort him)*

Matron   Thank God you've come, sir. I don't think he can go on like this much longer.

Nash   We came as soon as we could. How long has he been like this?

Christian   Nearly three days.

Nash   I'd no idea it was as bad as this.

Matron   It wasn't too bad at first, sir, just some gastric disturbance. Then all of a sudden this high fever, and the bleeding from the bowel and I'm sure I don't know how long this terrible pain can . . .

*(***Stephen*** *arches back, shrieks and dies)*

Mrs Nash   Stephen! Oh my God!!!

Make as varied a use as possible of the different media available to you.

4.11   Design: models

Any setting for a play is of course three-dimensional. It is therefore often dangerous to rely entirely on two-dimensional sketches and plans when designing a set. It is well worth taking time to construct a scale model of the set, and of any stage furniture, and painting it in the intended colours.

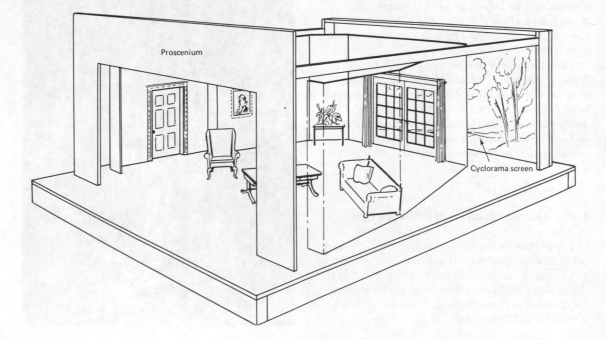

Proscenium

Cyclorama screen

Such a model will help in discussions with the director; it will help the actors visualise the area in which they will be performing, and, more importantly, it will allow you to check that entrances are in acceptable places, that there is room on stage for all necessary moves, and that no sight-lines are obscured. This means that no vital acting area is hidden from any part of the audience.

With the model you will be able to check with the lighting department that it will be possible to light the set. You must also check with the stage management team that the set will 'work' from their point of view – for example, that it will be possible to get each component onto the stage and that there are no impossible scene changes.

4.12 Period costume

The characters in Victorian Harlequinades (see 4.18) all had their own traditional costumes. These changed over the years. For example, originally, Harlequin wore a poor costume of patches and tatters. Gradually this changed into a smart suit of coloured diamond shapes.

Study different illustrations of the Harlequinade characters and design your own versions in which you can perform your project on this subject.

The fashion of a period reflects the ideas and attitudes of the period. Consider how 'Hell's Angels' dress. How smart people of the nineteen-twenties and thirties dressed. Or Elizabethan noblemen. What do their clothes tell us about the time in which they lived? What clothes do you think we shall be wearing in twenty years' time? Or in a hundred years' time? Try designing such clothes! What materials might be in use?

Consider the illustrations. What do they tell us about Victorian times? How would people move in such clothes? Improvise such costumes and rehearse the sorts of movements dictated by the clothes. Movements such as sitting, rising, turning, curtseying or bowing.

often easier to hire rather than make such
[ela]borate or tailored costumes. When hiring,
you must explain exactly what you want and
state the sizes required. It is worth getting
quotations from various hire–firms or from
theatres that hire out costumes – charges can
vary enormously.

Note that costumes will not arrive until the
last minute, which will give actors only a short
time to get used to them. Also remember that
the hirer may not supply footwear or other
accessories.

4.13   Lighting: colour

Coloured light can give a production *mood* or
atmosphere. It can be used to suggest warmth and
happiness or a gloom and sadness. More
dramatically it can create a rosy dawn, a ghostly
evening or the excitement of a disco or revue.

Colour filters are made from sheets of acetate,
and are sold under various trade names –
especially 'Cinemoid'. Nearly eighty colours are
available, each with its own number and,
sometimes rather odd, name. In the early stages,
work with a small range.

Begin with these three colours in a three–
circuit batten:

No 3 Straw,
No 17 Steel blue,
No 36 Pale lavender.

Adjust these until a natural light can be achieved
on a white cyclorama. Then experiment in using
pairs of colours from the group.

Now experiment with these three:

No 6 Primary red,
No 20 Deep blue,
No 39 Primary green.

What do they combine to produce? What is
achieved with any two of these? For what sort of
scenes would you use each of these six colours?

Try to achieve a sky effect that would suggest
– midday; dusk. Now create effects that suggest
a night club.

Another useful colour is No 31 Light frost.
This can be used in profile spots to soften their
impact.

As you become more ambitious, resist the
temptation to use a different colour in every
lantern. Select ones that match the scenery and
the costumes, and then rely on just one or two
shades of blue, pink, etc.

Some other useful colours include:

No 53	Pale salmon	warm, realistic colours;
No 54	Pale rose	warm, realistic colours;
No 50	Pale yellow	useful for sunlight, so too is No 3;
No 52	Pale gold	a warm golden colour;
No 47	Apricot	useful for suggesting warm interiors;
No 7	Light rose	a warm pinkish colour;
No 67	Steel tint	a cool colour, like No 17;
No 40	Pale blue	a stronger colour: quite cold;
No 63	Sky blue	useful for skies, a warmish blue;
No 19	Dark blue	a nightime colour.

Beware of using too much colour and so
muddling the effects and draining away all the
intensity of your lanterns. Remember too that in
most productions you will rely on white light,
keeping colour for adding subtlety and mood –
especially from the floodlights. Keep bright
colours for non–realistic settings.

Experiment to see what you can achieve – and
don't wait until the day before a production!

4.14   Sound control

The drawing illustrates a typical sound control
room from where can be played all disc and
taped effects. 'Live' spot effects must obviously
be created backstage – or wherever the script
dictates they should sound as though they are
happening.

Well before the technical rehearsal, the wise
sound engineer will compile a 'sound plot'
which lists all effects, together with their cues
and details of the level at which they should be
played.

Music before a performance starts can help
relax and 'warm–up' an audience. It can also help
maintain the atmosphere during any interval and
as the audience leaves – but note the points made

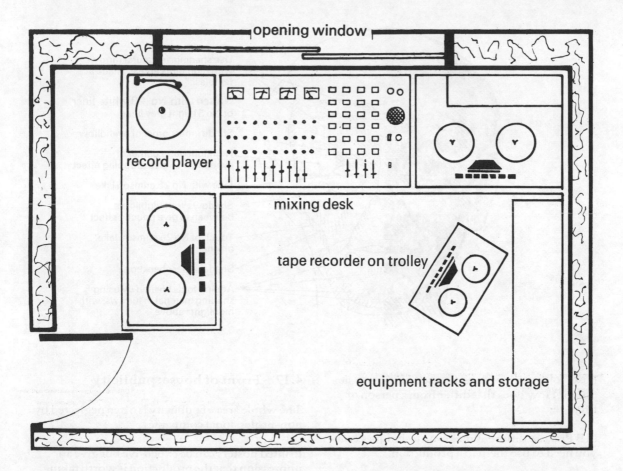

opening window

record player

mixing desk

tape recorder on trolley

equipment racks and storage

in this review of a school production of Peter Shaffer's play, *The Royal Hunt of the Sun*:

> The music and electronic effects also helped enormously to evoke atmosphere. However, I wish that the sound technicians would not play their favourite record selections before the play and during the interval. I spent the first ten minutes in my seat attempting to understand the significance of the 'Missa Luba' and 'Stranger on the Shore' to Shaffer's play. Properly chosen incidental music can so effectively prepare the audience for what is to follow.

4.15 Make-up: ageing

It is all too easy to overdo the application of make-up when trying to make a young face look old. It is far better to underdo it than to achieve a result that merely looks like a young person with a lot of red and white lines on his or her face!

Apply the foundation first – try 4½ or 6 mixed with 9. Then add the shadow areas under the eyebrows and eyes and under the chin – use 16. Brush eyebrows backwards with 5.

Now ask the actor to wrinkle up his face and then paint in the natural lines. Put some make-up on one palm and then use this as a palette, applying the make-up from your hand to the face with an orange stick. Lines should be drawn steadily and firmly, but as thinly as possible. Fade the ends of the lines so that they merge into the foundation.

Remember that make-up does not replace the need for acting. Age must be suggested by movement and speech – as well as by Leichner! Rehearse moving as people of different ages:

85

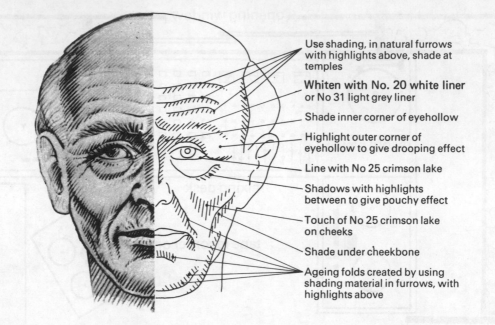

Use shading, in natural furrows with highlights above, shade at temples

Whiten with No. 20 white liner or No 31 light grey liner

Shade inner corner of eyehollow

Highlight outer corner of eyehollow to give drooping effect

Line with No 25 crimson lake

Shadows with highlights between to give pouchy effect

Touch of No 25 crimson lake on cheeks

Shade under cheekbone

Ageing folds created by using shading material in furrows, with highlights above

how, for example, does a person of seventy sit down? How does that differ from a person of fifty?

NB Practise different make-up techniques *before* you need to use them in a production.

4.16   Stagecraft: flats

Flats are rectangular wooden frames covered with stretched canvas. They are used to build box-sets and to mask the sides of stages, particularly proscenium stages, and are cleated or hinged together.

The top of the flats should normally be a metre higher than the top of the proscenium arch. Their framework is normally made from three by one wood, with proper joints at the corners. Before they are painted, new flats must be primed. Hardboard can be used instead of canvas – it is cheaper but makes the flats much heavier. Flats are supported by braces and weights.

Door and window flats are what they say they are – flats with windows and doorways cut into them.

4.17   Front of house: publicity

The whole area of publicity is often neglected by non-professional companies.

Printed posters can be expensive but give an impression that the production is worth taking seriously! Don't overcrowd them with information, remember they are useless if they cannot be read from a distance!

Hand-painted posters can be much more imaginative, and there are plenty of opportunities for liaison between a poster artist and the design department. These posters are particularly suitable for advertising school and college productions and can do a lot to stimulate interest in the coming show. Check though that they don't become so imaginative that the information they are meant to convey gets lost!

Handbills and hanging cards and the tickets themselves can also give useful publicity – as can the programme, if it is available in advance. Note that the programme should give the audience some background information about a play: any facts that are necessary to understand the situations it presents, the characters and theme, as well as details of the cast.

Particularly when staging an ambitious production or a 'home-made' play, it is often possible to gain a lot of useful publicity in the local press and on local radio, or even television stations. Victorian posters are illustrated above.

4.18 Project: Harlequinade

Originating in Italy, the *Commedia dell'Arte* was a popular form of theatre for two hundred years or more. The name *Commedia dell'Arte* means 'comedy of artists'.

Over the years, the details of the staging altered and by the nineteenth century it was known in England as 'Harlequinade' – and was still very popular. One reason for this was that the characters were always recognisable even though the situations in particular plays might vary. The audience knew that one character would always grumble, another would always fall in love, a third would be cheeky, and so on.

These are five of the main characters:

Harlequin

Sometimes a poor young man but often a servant, he is usually in love with Columbine. He can be cunning, and he is usually lazy. He wants to know everything he can about other people. He is able to sing, dance, juggle, skip, walk on his hands, walk on stilts, somersault, etc.

Columbine

She is usually the daughter of a rich man who is trying to marry her to one of his unattractive friends against her wishes. She loves to be loved. She loves Harlequin, but likes being courted by other men. She is a bit of a flirt.

Pantaloon

Pantaloon is an old man who loves money. He is selfish, bad-tempered and suspicious, especially with his servants. He moves about hunched up, glancing around suspiciously.

88

Pierrot

Pierrot is a servant. Unlike Harlequin, he seldom wins the girl he loves, but is left melancholy and alone.

El Capitano

El Capitano, 'the captain', is a boastful soldier who constantly boasts of his victories in battle and his success with women. He swaggers about, but in fact he is a coward and a constant failure with women.

Work on developing these characters and then act out a number of different stories involving them. For example, let Columbine be the daughter of Pantaloon, Pantaloon be trying to marry her off to el Capitano, and Columbine be hopelessly in love with Harlequin. Harlequin is too lazy to elope, so Pierrot has to find a way of helping the young lovers . . .

Or, on another occasion, el Capitano could be pretending love to Columbine in order to gain access to the house so he can steal Pantaloon's gold – which is later recovered by Harlequin.

Or you could do what became popular in the eighteenth and nineteenth centuries. That is, to re-tell traditional tales – The Sleeping Beauty, Aladdin, Cinderella, etc. – but cast them from the basic Harlequinade characters, adding to them as is necessary for the plot. Use reference books to find out about the other characters in the *Commedia dell' Arte* and Harlequinade.

The illustrations will give you some idea of the traditional costumes. Pierrot always wore a white costume, not unlike a clown suit, symbolising innocence. El Capitano wore black and Pantaloon red. Most of the characters usually wore masks, though Columbine never did – so that her great beauty was visible for all to see!

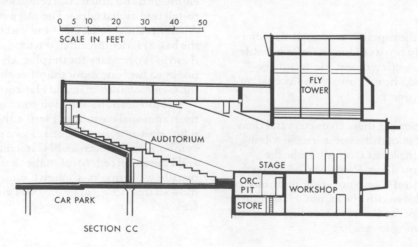

```
0  5  10    20    30    40    50
SCALE IN FEET
```

FLY
TOWER

AUDITORIUM

STAGE

ORC.
PIT

WORKSHOP

STORE

CAR PARK

SECTION CC

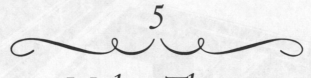

5

Modern Theatre

5.1 Modern stages

For two hundred years a single form of theatre, the proscenium stage, remained over-whelmingly popular. This century we have revived much older forms and experimented with new ones.

The opposite of the proscenium stage, with audience and actors firmly separated, is theatre-in-the-round. This requires a very different form of acting and establishes a strong relationship between actors and audience.

A compromise between the two is the open stage. Here the audience and actors are in the same 'room', there is no separating archway, but there is a chance to build more elaborate scenery than there is 'in-the-round', where it can easily obscure the audience's sight lines. A typical modern open-stage theatre is the Gateway at Chester, shown opposite and below.

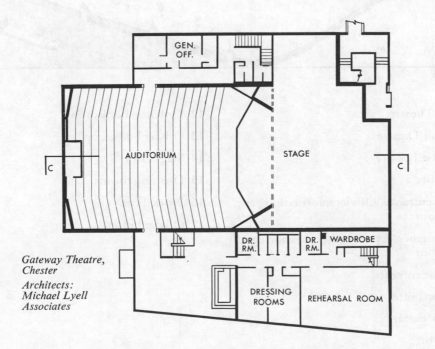

Gateway Theatre, Chester

Architects: Michael Lyell Associates

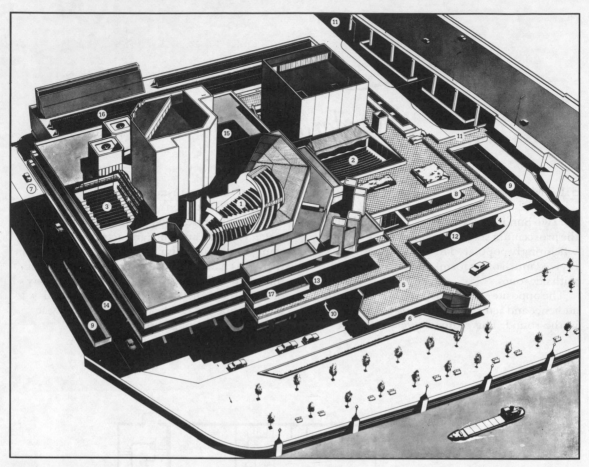

Key

1 Olivier Theatre

2 Lyttelton Theatre

3 Cottesloe Theatre

4 Box Office

5 Terrace entrance, Olivier information desk, cloakroom

6 Main entrance, Lyttelton information desk, cloakroom

7 Cottesloe entrance

8 Lyttelton buffet

9 Car park entrances

10 Restaurant

11 Exits to Waterloo station

12 Lyttelton bookshop

13 Olivier bookshop

14 Stage door

15 Dressing rooms

16 Workshops

17 Olivier buffet

5.2 The National Theatre

Few theatres are as large as or as complex as the National Theatre which stands on the south bank of the Thames in London, not far from where Shakespeare's theatre was.

It actually consists of three theatres. There is the Olivier Theatre – seating 1160 with an open stage; the Lyttelton – seating 890 with a proscenium stage; and the Cottesloe – seating anything between 200 and 400, depending on how the seats are arranged in this 'empty space'.

The diagram shows just what goes into a modern theatre complex.

5.3 Modern dramatists

Since 1955, there has been a great revival in the British theatre, with many new playwrights having their work performed.

Some of the most successful plays have been:

Samuel Beckett	*Waiting for Godot*
John Osborne	*Look Back in Anger*
Arnold Wesker	*Roots*
Willis Hall	*The Long and the Short and the Tall* (pictured below)
John Arden	*Serjeant Musgrave's Dance*
Robert Bolt	*A Man for All Seasons*
Harold Pinter	*The Caretaker*
Peter Shaffer	*The Royal Hunt of the Sun*
Tom Stoppard	*Rosencrantz and Guildenstern Are Dead*
Alan Ayckbourn	*The Norman Conquests*

Which plays would form *your* favourite 'top ten'?

5.4 Improvisation: play–making

When repeating an improvisation and developing it into a 'play' that is to be shown to an audience, these seven points should be kept in mind:

1. Before any 'run-through', all the members of a group should check they know the 'geography' of the scene – where is the front door and the fire-place; how is the furniture arranged?

2. Those taking part must agree on those facts that cannot be disputed. For example, members of a 'family' must know the ages of their children and stick to such facts during each improvisation.

3.   After each repetition of a scene, the whole group should discuss what went well, how else it could end and how it can be made more realistic. In such discussion, talk about the characters and how *they* behave, not about actors and how they perform.

4.   In discussion, develop and fill in the background of the characters involved. Age? Job? Hobbies and preoccupations? Ambitions? Previous disappointments or illnesses? Attitudes to each of the other characters?

5.   Keep asking 'What are we taking for granted?' 'What will an audience need to be told?'

6.   Don't allow it to get too long – there's a temptation to keep adding to it! Be prepared to cut parts out!

7.   Remember that in any run through or performance, you must 'accept' new points that may crop up, and that you must keep in character.

Now take a well-known pantomime story, such as Cinderella or Red Riding Hood or Aladdin, and make a modern documentary or 'realistic' play from it. To give you some ideas, this is how the satirical magazine *Private Eye* once reported the story of Snow White.

Action will be taken by the Government to ensure that the shocking story of Snow White will never be repeated.

Last night an eight million page report by a panel of seventy-three experts called for drastic changes in the laws concerning adoption, fostering, and the whole complex system of administration with regard to all aspects of child care.

The report singles out for special censure the notorious 'seven men of restricted growth' who obtained custody of the little girl.

These men, the committee states, had had no training in the techniques of child maintenance and should never have been allowed to supervise Snow White's welfare.

As a result of their 'culpable negligence' the child's step-mother gained illegal access to the dwarfs' dwelling and administered a fatal dose of poisoned apple to the little girl.

It was clearly shown that the seven dwarfs were in the habit of going out early in the morning whistling and singing, leaving the child alone and unattended for long periods of time. During the day Snow White was used by the dwarfs to perform domestic duties without any financial reimbursement.

Subsequent investigations have uncovered the fact that at least one dwarf, known simply as Dopey, suffered from 'a personality defect' as a result of which he became a state-registered drug addict.

5.5 Movement: from stage directions

Many modern dramatists include very precise directions to the actors and the director in their scripts. This is certainly the case with Harold Pinter (see 2.11). In his play *The Caretaker* there is a scene in which the three characters – Aston; Mick, his younger brother; and Davies, who is an old tramp – confront each other. Aston has just recovered Davies' bag from a café; Mick is intent on needling Davies.

Work on this scene until you can act it with the variety of pace intended by Pinter, and so that the movements are natural but also an accurate realisation of the script.

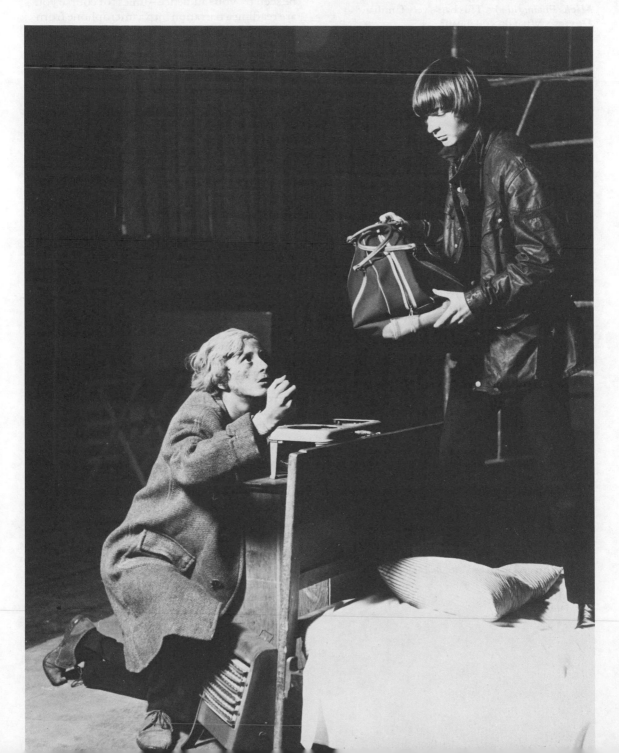

Aston (to **Davies**) I got your bag.

Davies Oh. (*Crossing to him and taking it*) Oh thanks, mister, thanks. Give it to you, did they?

(**Davies** *crosses back with the bag.* **Mick** *rises and snatches it*)

Mick What's this?

Davies Give us it, that's my bag!

Mick (*Warding him off*) I've seen this bag before.

Davies That's my bag!

Mick (*Eluding him*) This bag's very familiar.

Davies What do you mean?

Mick Where'd you get it?

Aston (*Rising, to them*) Scrub it.

Davies That's mine.

Mick Whose?

Davies It's mine! Tell him it's mine!

Mick This your bag?

Davies Give me it!

Aston Give it to him.

Mick What? Give him what?

Davies That bloody bag!

Mick (*Slipping it behind the gas stove*) What bag? (*To* **Davies**) What bag?

Davies (*Moving*) Look here!

Mick (*Facing him*) Where you going?

Davies I'm going to get . . . my old . . .

Mick Watch your step, sonny! You're knocking at the door when no one's at home. Don't push it too hard. You come busting into a private house, laying your hands on anything you can lay your hands on. Don't overstep the mark, son.
(**Aston** *picks up the bag.*)

Davies You thieving bastard . . . you thieving skate . . . let me get my –

Aston Here you are. (**Aston** *offers the bag to* **Davies.** **Mick** *grabs it.* **Aston** *takes it.* **Mick** *grabs it.* **Davies** *reaches for it.* **Aston** *takes it.* **Mick** *reaches for it.* **Aston** *gives it to* **Davies.** **Mick** *grabs it. Pause.*

Aston *takes it.* **Davies** *takes it.* **Mick** *takes it.* **Davies** *reaches for it. Pause.*

Aston *gives it to* **Mick.** **Mick** *gives it to* **Davies.** **Davies** *grasps it to him. Pause.*

Mick *looks at* **Aston.** **Davies** *moves away with the bag. He drops it. Pause. They watch him. He picks it up. Goes to his bed, and sits.* **Aston** *goes to his bed, sits, and begins to roll a cigarette.* **Mick** *stands still. Pause.*)

5.6 Public–speaking

Occasionally you will have to read aloud in public or deliver a speech. Remember these points:

It is very much easier to read or speak from a standing position and from one where you can be seen by your audience – unless of course you are reading a narration into a microphone from an off stage position.

If reading, do rehearse – don't try to sight-read.

If delivering a talk, don't try to remember it word by word – remember its main points.

If you are using a microphone, rehearse with it. Don't try to use it as a pop singer might. (See 5.14).

Concentrate on the *sense* of what you are reading or saying.

Speak to the audience – think of them. Don't just launch words into space.

Don't be afraid to gesture when it is helpful.

Vary the volume, pace, pitch and tone as the sense dictates.

Don't be afraid to pause.

Now work on this speech. The secretary is secretary of a Northern social and entertainment club. He is on a small stage, talking to an audience busy drinking and chattering among themselves.

Secretary And now, ladies and gentlemen, your kind attention, please . . . (*the noise barely alters*) I'm waiting for your kind attention, ladies and gentlemen . . . I don't want to wait all night. Thank you . . . (*Quiet*) . . . As announced in last week's club bulletin, there will now be a brief interval in the bingo . . . (*Groans, calls of 'No'*) . . . it's been announced, it's been announced . . . a brief interval in the bingo to listen to some new comics setting their feet on the first rung of the ladder of fame. Now this'll last half an hour at the most and I'd like you to show these lads the traditional courtesy of the club and then we'll get straight back to bingo as soon as it's over. So I think we're in for a treat. . . . First off then, a young man from Ireland, now domiciled in Moss Side, your welcome please for . . . Mick . . . Connor.

Elaine Stritch speaking at a presentation

That scene comes from a play by Trevor Griffiths called *Comedians*. Following that speech, a number of would-be comedians perform their acts, with varying degrees of success, to the audience.

Some of your group might develop their own comic, or musical, 'turns', and you could stage your own variety show.

Practise your timing – note which jokes, stories and other items will go well. Perform to your audience. Learn from their reactions.

5.7 Acting: performance

On the day or evening of a performance, always arrive at the theatre in good time – don't come rushing in at the last moment.

Put on make-up carefully and patiently.

Check that the details of your costume are correct and that any necessary props are in your pockets.

When not on stage, don't crowd the wings and get in the way of the stage crew.

On stage, concentrate. Listen, and react to the other actors as you have rehearsed.

Speak up well; don't start to gabble if you feel nervous.

Don't panic over mistakes – stay in character. Accept prompts in character.

Be alert for laughter or other reactions. Hold your position and start again as the sound begins to fade. Don't wait for silence or the pace will flag.

Don't be put off by different reactions from different audiences.

Don't alter things decided in rehearsal.

Don't over-act for laughs.

Be ready to take part in assessment discussions after a production. Consider the comments that are made and decide which you can learn from.

5.8   Mime show

By now, you should be able to put together a programme of mime items. Think about the running order: try to achieve a balance of solo and group items; items performed in silence and those accompanied by music; sad and comic ones.

You might devise one based on this excerpt from *Gulliver's Travels* by Jonathan Swift. Gulliver has been shipwrecked in the land of Brobdingnag, a land populated by giants, men as tall as church steeples. He hides near a cornfield, where some of the giants are harvesting the corn.

> One of the reapers, approaching within ten yards of the ridge where I lay, made me apprehend that with the next step I should be squashed to death under his foot, or cut in two with his reaping-hook. And therefore when he was about to move, I screamed as loud as fear could make me.

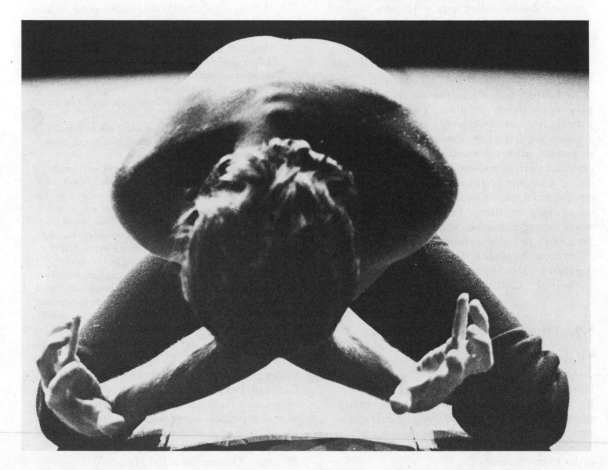

Whereupon the huge creature trod short, and looking round about under him for some time, at last espied me as I lay on the ground. He considered a while with the caution of one who endeavours to lay hold on a small dangerous animal in such a manner that it shall not be able either to scratch or to bite him. At length he ventured to take me up behind by the middle between his forefinger and thumb, and brought me within three yards of his eyes, that he might behold my shape more perfectly.

I resolved not to struggle in the least as he held me in the air above sixty foot from the ground, although he grievously pinched my sides, for fear I should slip through his fingers. All I ventured was to raise mine eyes towards the sun and place my hands together in a supplicating posture.

I apprehended every moment that he would dash me against the ground, as we usually do any little hateful animal which we have a mind to destroy. But he appeared pleased with my gestures, and began to look upon me as a curiosity.

In the meantime I was not able to forbear groaning and shedding tears, and turning my head towards my sides; letting him know, as well as I could, how cruelly I was hurt by the pressure of his thumb and finger. He seemed to apprehend my meaning; for lifting up a pocket of his coat, he put me gently into it.

In the first instance, mime it as a solo item, playing the part of the giant. Then mime it, playing the part of Gulliver.

Now work in pairs, some distance apart. One of you is Gulliver, the other is the giant. Co-ordinate your actions and reactions, so that you give the impression that, although you are both similar sizes, one of you is really a giant, the other a tiny creature. At first you will need to work facing each other. Later you will be able to perform it facing the audience. It will be very effective if the stage is dark, except for two quite separate pools of light. In one, we see the giant; in the other, Gulliver.

5.9 Directing: modern theories

There have been many varied theories about directing plays in recent years. One of the famous directors this century was a Russian, Konstantin Stanislavsky. In fact, he had many theories about acting. One thing he did believe very strongly was that an actor must use his imagination to recall exactly how it was – in order to re-create it:

If I ask you a perfectly simple question now, 'Is it cold out today?' before you answer, even with a 'yes', or 'it's not cold', or 'I didn't notice', you should, in your imagination, go back onto the street and remember how you walked or rode. You should test your sensations by remembering how the people you met were wrapped up, how they turned up their collars, how the snow crunched underfoot, and only then can you answer my question.

In his book *An Actor Prepares*, he writes of a director teaching an actor through mime exercises:

'We have had enough of theory,' said the director when he began work today. 'Let us put some of it into practice.' Whereupon he called on me to go up on the stage and play the exercise of burning the money. 'I shall give you neither real nor property money. Working with air will compel you to bring back more details, and build a better sequence. If every little auxiliary act is executed truthfully, then the whole action will unfold rightly.'

I began to count the non–existent bank notes.

'I don't believe it,' said Tortsov, stopping me as I was just reaching for the money.

'What don't you believe?'

'You did not even look at the thing you were touching.'

I had looked over to the make-believe piles of bills, seen nothing; merely stretched out my arm and brought it back.

'If only for the sake of appearances you might press your fingers together so that the packet won't fall from them. Don't throw it down. Put it down. And who would undo a package that way? First find the end of the string. No, not like that. It cannot be done so suddenly. The ends are tucked in carefully, so that they do not come loose. It is not easy to untangle them. That's right,' he said approvingly at last. 'Now count the hundreds first, there are usually ten of them to a packet. Oh, dear! How quickly you did all that! Not even the most expert cashier could have counted those crumpled, dirty old banknotes at such a rate!'

The moment I was convinced of the truth of my physical actions, I felt perfectly at ease on the stage.

Other famous directors have included the German, Bertolt Brecht; and there have been many famous English directors in the last few years – especially Peter Brook, famous for his production of *A Midsummer Night's Dream* (see 5.11); and Peter Hall, the director of the National Theatre from 1973 (see 5.2).

Sir Peter Hall directing a rehearsal

5.10 Documentary: making a point

A dramatised documentary, be it on film or on stage, can be an impressive way of conveying information or a forceful way of making a point (see 1.10).

Use the photograph on the following page as the starting point for researching and presenting a documentary on refugees, or the following items from the *Daily Mirror* as the basis of one on truancy.

In either case try to present up-to-date information about the problem and its causes, and, in dramatised scenes, suggest what it is like to be a refugee or truant.

Every week, more than a million British children play truant. Paul is one of them. He's thirteen. This is his scene.

If you really want the details he's turned up at his secondary school on 112 days out of a possible 476.

'I usually didn't turn up,' he says disarmingly, 'but sometimes I wandered off between classes. Y'know?'

His Mum works in a factory canteen and when she leaves their London suburban semi in the morning, Paul goes with her. They part company at the park gates and he cuts smartly into the kids' playground.

At ten o'clock he goes 'up West'. He used to fool around in the High Street, but that was when his Mum didn't know he was on the wag – playing

truant. Now she gives him 50p a day and he gets the train to Charing Cross.

And the rest is where his fancy takes him: just looking, or the arcades, or the pictures, and sometimes train-spotting. He has to be careful: the coppers get nosey in term time.

A quarter of a million kids get that walled-in feeling every week in Britain and stay away – seven in every ten, incidentally, covered by a note from mum or dad. Another million of them sneak out after checking in for early morning 'register'.

5.11 Design: planning a production

This is a summary of the various processes the design department must work through or supervise during a production:

reading and study of the text;
research into the period;
discussion with the director;
more research;
production of rough sketches;

Model set for A Midsummer Night's Dream *produced by Peter Brook (1970)*

more discussion;
making a model of the set;
check with all departments;
revisions;
· building;
painting;
preparation of the stage floor and installation of set;
check for stability;
touching up of paintwork, etc.

NB All sets must comply with local fire regulations and, if necessary, must be fire-proofed. It is well-worth contacting your local safety officer in the early stages of planning, and obtaining a guide called *Play Safe*, issued by the Greater London Council, County Hall, S.E.1.

5.12 Costume: the performance

During the run of a production, even if it is a single studio performance, the jobs of whoever is in charge of the costumes can be divided up as follows:

At dress rehearsals:
Note any alterations and additions that have become necessary, for example, do any actors now need belts or hats or gloves; need any hemlines be adjusted or waistbands let out? Check that the designer and director are happy with the costumes.

Make sure that the cast understand that *they* are now responsible for their own costumes till after the show. Insist that they hang them up after use, and that they hand anything to you that needs washing, ironing or mending after a particular performance.

If any actor has a quick change of costume, insist that he or she rehearses it. Decide where the change will take place during the show.
During the performance:
Check that costumes are correct before each actor goes on stage for the first time.
Have plenty of safety pins, needle and thread, scissors, etc. with you at all times.
It may also be useful to have a hair brush and comb and a small mirror with you, plus a clothes brush.

103

After the production is over:
Sort and check costumes.
Return items that have been borrowed from individuals, and write thank you letters.
Return hired costumes.
Clean, mend and pack away costumes owned by the company. Give any accounts to the business manager.

5.13   Lighting: plot and rehearsal

The lighting designer should be involved in the early planning of a production. He should certainly see the model of the set and attend at least some rehearsals.

With the director, designer and stage manager, he will work out the lighting plot. This lists all the lighting cues. Lighting cues are *changes* in the lighting. The *cue* is the start of the change, the *cue time* is the number of seconds it takes to happen, and the *cue state* is the state of the lighting after the change has happened.

Never indulge in cues for their own sakes. They should be dictated by the plot and the audience should recognise them only when necessary and then only after they have happened. At the end of a performance the audience should be talking about the play and the actors – not about the lighting changes!

Positioning of lanterns, rigging and focusing should all be finished in time to allow for a lighting rehearsal before any technical rehearsal.

104

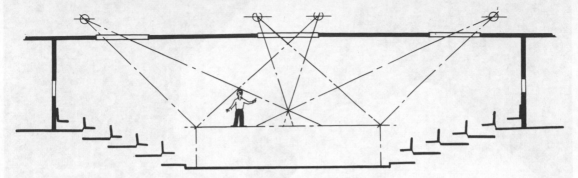

NB The lighting of thrust stages and theatres–in–the–round can cause some problems. The lanterns must be positioned so that they do not light the audience, nor so that they light only the top of the actors' heads. See the diagram.

5.14 Tape-recording

Whether tape-recording sound effects or speech for use in a stage play or when recording a play on tape, the following points may be helpful:

1.   Discover the directional qualities of your microphone – that is, from how wide an angle it picks up sound.

2.   Even the best microphone cannot produce a good recording over a long distance from the sound source. For speech, it should be 30–40 cm from the mouth. Obviously those readers with stronger voices can be further away than those who do not project well.

3.   It is much easier to record a play with the actors standing rather than sitting. They can then easily tiptoe away when not involved in a dialogue, and so allow those that are speaking to stand in the best position.

4.   Don't hold the script between mouth and microphone, and avoid rustling pages.

5.   Rooms with bare walls are unsuitable for recording in, as they have a very echo–y sound. Where possible, use a carpeted, curtained room – unless of course an echo–y effect is required!

6.   It is possible to minimise echo, and also to lessen background noise, by speaking closer to the microphone and by turning down the recording level. When doing this, a better sound may be achieved by speaking across the microphone rather than directly into it.

7.   Gently fading out the very first few words or sounds of a scene and fading in the first sounds of a new scene will suggest a transition from one scene to another.

The photographs illustrate how reel–to–reel tape may be edited.

Marking the cutting place with a chinagraph pencil

Above: Cutting the tape with a razor-blade

Below: Joining the ends with adhesive tape

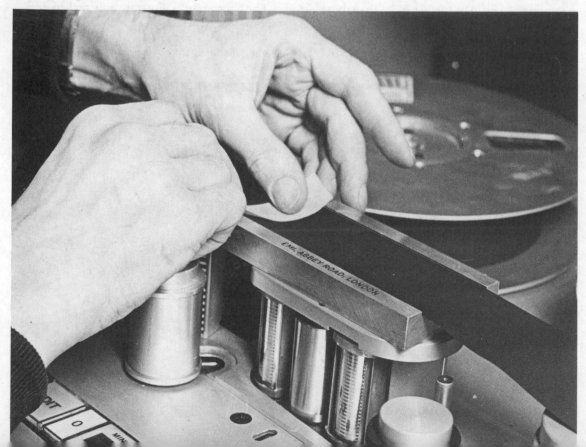

The following excerpt comes from a radio play devised for a school drama group. Called *Ring-a-king*, it updated the story of the birth of Christ, and re-told it entirely by telephone calls. Using it as a model, try devising your own 'tape' play. Alternatively, try recording this scene. A 'distant' telephone voice can be created with the help of a paper cup. (NB: *FX – sound effects*)

(Fade in on:
FX   *Gusty wind [outdoor acoustic]*
   Hold behind.)
Balthazar   Well, if we're lost we'll have to ring up, won't we? There's a phone box there.
Caspar   All right, all right. I heard you. Look, I'll open the door for you. You do it.
FX   *(Door opens and closes; decrease wind)*
Balthazar   I'll find out his number first.
FX   *(Receiver lifted; dialling three digits; number ringing)*
Operator *(Distant)*   Enquiries, can I help you?
Balthazar   Ah. Hello. I was wondering if you could possibly give me the number of King Herod.
Operator *(Distant)*   Which town?
Balthazar   Well, Jerusalem of course. King Herod, surely you know him?
Operator *(Distant)*   Well, I'm new to the area . . . let me see, 'H' for Herod, or is it 'K' for king? No, Kings are in yellow pages. 'H' . . . er, Henry . . . Herbert . . . yes, here we are, Herod, you did say Herod, didn't you?
Balthazar   Yes I did. Number?
Operator *(Distant)*   3589622.
Balthazar   3 . . 5 . . 8 . . 9 . . 6 . . 22. Right. Thank you.
FX   *(Receiver down; receiver picked up; dialling seven digits; phone rings other end.*
   Fade down.
   Fade in on.
FX   *Trimphone ringing. Receiver picked up.)*
Butler   Herod's Palace.
FX   *(STD Paytone, coins in slot.)*
Balthazar *(Distant)*   Ah, could I possibly have a word with His Majesty King Herod, please? I'm King Balthazar of the Orient.
Butler   What is your business, sire?
Balthazar *(Distant)*   It's an urgent matter, about the birth of a king.
Butler   I'll see if he's free, sire.
Herod   I'm standing behind you. Here, give me the phone. What's all this about a new king?
Balthazar *(Distant)*   Am I speaking to King Herod?
Herod   You are! Now what's all this nonsense?
Balthazar *(Distant)*   My colleagues and I are trying to locate the town of Bethlehem but we seem to have taken the wrong road.

Herod   What could possibly interest you in Bethlehem?
Balthazar *(Distant)*   A new king'll be born there very soon.
Herod   Impossible! I am the king! That's an impertinent suggestion!
Balthazar *(Distant)*   Our information is most reliable.
Herod   Well! . . . well, in that case, I should like to see him myself. Where are you ringing from?
Balthazar *(Distant)*   A call-box overlooking the Dead Sea.
Herod   You've travelled too far south, just take the road from the northern shore and you'll find it signposted after about four hours travelling.
Balthazar *(Distant)*   Thank you for your assistance.
FX *(Distant)*   *(Paytone)*
Herod   Now, can I rely on yours? Will you ring me again as soon as you can after finding this . . . er . . . king? You won't forget, will you? I'm most interested . . .
FX   *(Dialling tone, receiver down.)*
Herod   Operator, try to trace that call, will you?
   (Fade down.)

5.15   Make-up: eccentrics

Devising make-up for sub-humans, monsters and aliens is where the imagination can come into its own. The main rule is to experiment!

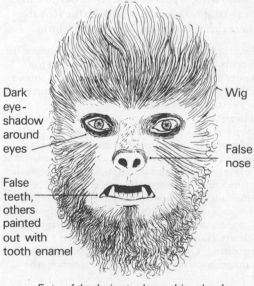

Dark eye-shadow around eyes

Wig

False nose

False teeth, others painted out with tooth enamel

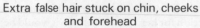

Extra false hair stuck on chin, cheeks and forehead

107

The following points may be helpful:
1. Metallic sprays can be used on well–greased skin – but *always* protect the eyes and hair; 57 Gold and 58 Silver are also useful for suggesting non–humans or aliens.
2. Use 5 as a foundation for ghosts, etc.
3. Use 5 mixed with green for witches.
4. Use tooth enamel to black out individual teeth.
5. Stage blood is available in gelatine capsules which can be kept in the mouth and broken when required; or in bottles. For 'stabbings' a small quantity should be sealed up in a cellophane bag, and carefully pricked when required. The bag can be stuck to the skin with a piece of sticking plaster.
6. Whip marks and lashes can be created by daubing finger tips with 9, and then pulling the fingers across the area to be marked.
Try creating make–up for these characters:
    a witch;
    a hobbit;
    an elf;
    an alien from outer space;
    an ill–treated convict.

5.16 Stage–management

The following is part of an account of the work of an assistant stage manager with the Royal Shakespeare Company, Maggie Whitlum:

> Her first job was as an assistant stage manager at the Phoenix Theatre in Leicester, which led on to a deputy's job in Coventry. Before her recent move to the RSC she was a fully–fledged stage manager at the Nottingham Playhouse.
> Rehearsals are the best part of the job, says Maggie. She is responsible for getting the rehearsal room ready and organising any furniture or costumes required. She is also 'on the book' which means that she is responsible for keeping up during rehearsals a master copy of the play. In it are entered all the actors' moves as they are decided, all the cues for lighting and music, plots for furniture and props in each scene, and standbys for actors and stage-crew. Rehearsal is a time of experimenting and organising. Once the first night is over, the stage manager's job on that play is just repetition, she says.
> That is why a job in the West End theatre holds no attraction for her. 'On a long run it would be

terrible – in at six each evening doing the same routine, no company atmosphere.'
Stage managers have to check that all doors or windows supposed to open do so, and set out the props for the first act, whisky, roses, sheets, books. She has also been responsible for prompting, but has only given one in four years.

During the later rehearsals, the technical and dress rehearsals, and the performances, it is the stage manager who is in charge of all that happens on stage. It is his job to co-ordinate the lighting and sound effects, to see that furniture and properties are in place, to supervise any scenery changes – and to be responsible for the discipline of the cast both on stage or off.

One of his assistants will be the prompter, like Maggie Whitlum. Some groups do without a prompter – insisting that the cast improvise their way back to the script. Whether you have a prompter or not depends on the way your group works and on the play. It is easier to improvise in the middle of a documentary or modern play than in the middle of a passage of Shakespearean verse for example!

If you do have a prompter, the following points should be observed:
1. Familiarise yourself with the whole play.
2. Incorporate each line or word change into the prompt book.
3. Familiarise yourself with the individual actor's approach to his part, and note the parts where he is unsure of his lines.
4. Learn to recognise each actor's private distress signals!
5. Give prompts speedily in the tone usually employed by the actor.
6. Expect actors to dry where they have *never* had any trouble before!
7. Learn how much volume you need to use. Better to be heard by the audience than not heard by the actor.
8. Keep a torch handy.

5.17 The audience

The most difficult part of any production to get right is the audience: they are the one part it is impossible to rehearse. If they respond critically or if they become restless, it is not their fault. Something is wrong with the production – even

if it is only a matter of its not being the right production for that audience.

Begin by giving small, informal presentations. Don't switch suddenly from improvised drama shown only within the group to a full-scale public performance.

Have the courage to show your own 'home-made' projects to audiences – but make sure they know what they are in for and what your aims are in each particular presentation. If presented at the right time and in the right place, the showing of creative drama can be an electrifying experience for participants and audience. Even a cynical staffroom audience can be excited by the insight into the creative process, and an audience of friends and relatives can be fascinated by what they get drawn into. Certainly the outcome will not be the condescending 'Well, they're very good for their age' which is the response to some indifferent school and college plays.

Whatever the presentation, try to make an occasion of it for the audience. In charge of this is the house manager, who may be also the producer. He is the host for the evening. He may not be able to change the school hall into the Theatre Royal for the night, but he can do quite a lot to help in advance. For example, he should:
1.   see that correctly worded invitations go out well in advance to those who should receive them;
2.   see that the box-office, or its equivalent, functions smoothly; that those who are selling or issuing tickets know what the play is about and can talk about it intelligently;
3.   tidy up the hall or theatre and cover up irrelevant posters and notices;
4.   number seats clearly; reserve seats for the press, if required, and for visiting dignitaries;
5.   decorate the foyer or other areas with floral arrangements.

On the night, he is in charge of those supervising car-parking, the cloakroom attendants, programme sellers, ticket collectors, ushers and usherettes, and those responsible for refreshments. He also co-ordinates the house lights with the stage manager.

5.18   Project: *The Last Flower*

The Last Flower is a fable by James Thurber, told in a series of cartoon drawings. Devise and stage a presentation based on the fable, using as many theatrical forms and devices as you think suitable. For example, you might rely on story-teller-plus-mime; you might fully dramatise the story, or you could present it as a documentary. NB In the original, each 'line' is illustrated by a separate drawing.

World War XII, as everybody knows, brought about the collapse of civilization.

Towns, cities, and villages disappeared from the earth.

All the groves and forests were destroyed,
    and all the gardens,
    and all the works of art.

Men, women, and children became lower than the lower animals.

Discouraged and disillusioned, dogs deserted their fallen masters.

Emboldened by the pitiful condition of the former lords of the earth, rabbits descended upon them.

Books, paintings, and music disappeared from the earth, and human beings just sat around doing nothing.

Years and years went by.

Even the few Generals who were left forgot what the last war had decided.

Boys and girls grew up to stare at each other blankly, for love had passed from the earth.

One day a young girl who had never seen a flower
  chanced to come upon the last one in the world.
She told the other human beings that the last flower
  was dying.
The only one who paid any attention to her was a
  young man she found wandering about.
Together the young man and the girl nurtured the
  flower and it began to live again.
One day a bee visited the flower, and a
  hummingbird.
Before long there were two flowers, and then four,
  and then a great many.
Groves and forests flourished again.
The young girl began to take an interest in how she
  looked.
The young man discovered that touching the girl
  was pleasurable.
Love was reborn into the world.
Their children grew up strong and healthy and
  learned to run and laugh.
Dogs came out of their exile.
The young man discovered, by putting one stone
  upon another, how to build a shelter.
Pretty soon everybody was building shelters.
Towns, cities, and villages sprang up.

Song came back into the world,
And troubadours and jugglers
And tailors and cobblers
And painters and poets
And sculptors and wheelwrights
And soldiers
And Lieutenants and Captains
And Generals and Major–Generals
And liberators.
Some people went one place to live, and some
  another.
Before long, those who went to live in the valleys
  wished they had gone to live in the hills,
And those who had gone to live in the hills wished
  they had gone to live in the valleys.
The liberators, under the guidance of God, set fire
  to the discontent,
So presently the World was at war again.
This time the destruction was so complete . . .
That nothing at all was left in the World –
Except one man
And one woman
And one flower.

James Thurber

Theatrical Terms

apron stage	permanent, or temporary, acting area in front of the proscenium
aside	speech delivered to the audience, supposedly not heard by the other characters on stage
backcloth	canvas with wooden beams at the top and bottom, on which can be painted scenery
blacks	black curtain serving as backdrop
borders	strips of cloth above stage, concealing anything above the stage from the audience's view
call	a request for actors to appear – as in 'photo-call', 'costume call'
comedy	play which creates laughter, one that ends happily
downstage	the part of the acting area nearest the audience
farce	play with ridiculous and improbable characters and actors, a very funny play
flies (or flytower)	space above the scenery or setting, where scenery can be hung or 'flown' when not in use
front of house (FOH)	auditorium, foyer, etc.
gels	coloured filters placed in spotlights and floodlights
ground plan	scale plan of set, viewed from above
house lights	lights in the auditorium
OP side	'opposite the prompter'; traditionally the prompter sits stage left, therefore stage right
PS side	prompter's side, stage left
raked stage	stage sloping upwards away from the audience
scene bay	space where scenery is stored
stage left	as an actor faces the audience, the left hand side of the stage
stage right	ditto, right hand side
strike	to dismantle a set
tabs	curtains
tragi-comedy	play which combines comedy and tragedy
trap	opening cut in stage floor, trap door
upstage	the part of the acting area furthest from the audience, see 1.7

Addresses

The following addresses may prove useful. Any group or company would do well to build up its own lists of contacts.

Art materials .... Winsor and Newton Ltd,
51–52 Rathbone Place,
London W1.

Books and scripts .... Samuel French Ltd,
P.O. Box 64
26 Southampton Street,
London WC2E 7JE.

Costume hire .... Royal Shakespeare Company,
(Costume hire department),
Royal Shakespeare Theatre,
Stratford–upon–Avon,
Warwickshire CV37 6BB.

also many regional and local repertory companies.

See also under 'Theatrical Costumiers' in Yellow Pages.

Make-up .... Leichner (London) Ltd,
436 Essex Road,
London N1 3PL.

Stage furnishing .... Hall & Dixon Ltd,
19 Garrick Street,
London WC2 9AX.

Stage lighting .... Rank Strand Electronic,
P.O. Box 70
Great West Road,
Brentford,
Middlesex TW8 9HR.

See also Yellow Pages

References

The following books will be useful for further reference on particular subjects and, together, would make an excellent theatre library. Most are fully illustrated.

Concise Oxford Companion to the Theatre, Phyllis Hartnoll (Oxford 1978)

Penguin Dictionary of the Theatre, John Russell Taylor (Penguin 1966)

A Handbook of the Theatre, Esmé Crampton (Heinemann Educational 1973)

Theatres, Simon Tidworth (Pall Mall Press 1973)

The Actor and His Body, Litz Pisk (Harrap 1975)

Voice and the Actor, Cicely Berry (Harrap 1973)

Designing and Making Stage Scenery, Michael Warre (Studio Vista 1966)

Designing and Making Stage Costumes, Motley (Studio Vista 1964)

Historic Costume for the Stage, Lucy Barton (A. & C. Black 1961)

Making Costumes for School Plays, Joan Peters and Anna Sutcliffe (Batsford 1977)

The Stage Lighting Handbook, Francis Reed (Pitman 1976)

Stage Sound, David Collison (Studio Vista 1976)

Stage Make-up for the School Play, Eric Jones (Batsford 1969)

Stage Crafts, Chris Hoggett (A. & C. Black 1975)

Amateur Drama: production and management, Martyn Hepworth (Batsford 1978)

A Practical Guide to Drama in the Secondary School, David Self (Ward Lock Educational 1975)

Stagecraft ed. Trevor R. Griffiths (Phaidon 1982)

Index

119